法律英语证书（LEC）全国统一考试
考 试 大 纲

法律英语证书（LEC）全国统一考试指导委员会　编

图书在版编目（CIP）数据

法律英语证书（LEC）全国统一考试考试大纲 / 法律英语证书（LEC）全国统一考试指导委员会编 . —北京：北京大学出版社，2019.5
　ISBN 978-7-301-30485-3

　Ⅰ.①法… Ⅱ.①法… Ⅲ.①法律—英语—统一考试—考试大纲 Ⅳ.① D9-41

中国版本图书馆 CIP 数据核字（2019）第 079712 号

书　　名	法律英语证书（LEC）全国统一考试考试大纲	
	FALÜ YINGYU ZHENGSHU (LEC) QUANGUO TONGYI KAOSHI KAOSHI DAGANG	
著作责任者	法律英语证书（LEC）全国统一考试指导委员会　编	
责任编辑	刘文静	
标准书号	ISBN 978-7-301-30485-3	
出版发行	北京大学出版社	
地　　址	北京市海淀区成府路 205 号　100871	
网　　址	http://www.pup.cn　　新浪微博：@ 北京大学出版社	
电子邮箱	编辑部 pupwaiwen@pup.cn　　总编室 zpup@pup.cn	
电　　话	邮购部 010-62752015　发行部 010-62750672	
	编辑部 010-62754382	
印 刷 者	北京虎彩文化传播有限公司	
经 销 者	新华书店	
	650 毫米 × 980 毫米　16 开本　11.75 印张　200 千字	
	2019 年 5 月第 1 版　2024 年 4 月第 5 次印刷	
定　　价	30.00 元	

未经许可，不得以任何方式复制或抄袭本书之部分或全部内容。
版权所有，侵权必究
举报电话：010-62752024 电子邮箱：fd@pup.pku.edu.cn
图书如有印装质量问题，请与出版部联系，电话：010-62756370

目 录

法律英语证书（LEC）全国统一考试考试大纲 ………………………… 1
    第一部分　考试说明 ……………………………………………… 1
    第二部分　考试内容 ……………………………………………… 2
    第三部分　考试形式 ……………………………………………… 6
    第四部分　考试题型及考核目标 ………………………………… 6
    第五部分　试题结构示例 ………………………………………… 7
    第六部分　考试样题及参考答案 ………………………………… 8

附录一　2018年11月法律英语证书（LEC）全国统一考试试题及
         参考答案 …………………………………………………… 76

附录二　常用法律英语词汇及术语 ………………………………… 143

法律英语证书（LEC）全国统一考试
考 试 大 纲

第一部分 考试说明

本考试是法律英语证书（Legal English Certificate，简称 LEC）水平考试，旨在测试并认定应试人员的法律英语语言水平与实际运用法律英语处理涉外法务的能力。法律英语证书（LEC）全国统一考试是为国内公检法机关和企事业单位、各类律师事务所、跨国公司等单位招募法律英语复合型人才和科学衡量高等学校和科研机构的涉外法学专业和法律英语专业学生的法律英语语言应用水平而设置的。它的评价标准是高等学校涉外法学专业和法律英语专业优秀本科毕业生能达到的及格或及格以上水平，以保证通过 LEC 考试者具有较好的法律英语语言应用水平，能够胜任包括法律翻译在内的涉外法律服务工作。

1. 本大纲依据涉外律师业务或国际法务从业人员工作内容分析结果编制，是法律英语证书全国统一考试的依据。

2. 考试对象
（1）公检法机关和企事业单位从事涉外法务的工作人员；
（2）从事涉外法务的律师、公司法律部门的从业人员；
（3）高等院校法律、英语、经贸、外交、国际政治等专业学生；
（4）愿意从事法律英语教学、测试及相关科研工作的人员；
（5）社会上一切法律英语爱好者。

3. 通过本考试能让应试者初步掌握涉外律师业务或国际法务各环节的英语语言表达能力、案例阅读理解能力、法律翻译及撰写涉外法律文书的技能。考试范围包括美国法律的基本知识和法律英语的读、写、译等方面的知识及技能。

4. 本大纲知识点按照法律英语证书（LEC）全国统一考试指定教材体例编排。

5. 考试指定推荐参考用书

（1）《法律英语精读教程》（上、下），北京大学出版社2016年版；

（2）《法律英语写作教程》，北京大学出版社2016年版；

（3）《法律英语翻译教程》，北京大学出版社2016年版；

（4）《法律英语泛读教程》（上、下），北京大学出版社2016年版；

（5）《大学法律英语》，北京大学出版社2018年版；

（6）《英美法律文化教程》，北京大学出版社2018年版；

（7）《大学法律英语教程》，外语教学与研究出版社2014年版；

（8）《大学法律英语高级教程》，外语教学与研究出版社2015年版。

6. 考试时间

本考试实行计算机考试，每年举行两次，分别在每年五月和十一月的最后一个星期六举行。每次考试时间为六个小时，上午三个小时为客观题（PART ONE），下午三个小时为主观题（PART TWO）。

有关考试最新动态，请考生随时关注LEC考试官方网站：www.lectest.com；咨询电话：010-58908397

第二部分　考试内容

一、法律基本知识

1. 常用法律英语词汇、术语的定义、内涵
2. 英美法律文化
3. 美国部门法

宪法 CONSTITUTIONAL LAW

The Judicial Power

Legislative Power

Executive Power

Individual Guarantees against Governmental or Private Action
Due Process
Equal Protection
Fundamental Rights
The First Amendment

合同法 CONTRACTS

Basics of Contracts
Contract Formation
Capacity of a Contract
Vitiating Factors
Problems Involving Persons other than the Parties to the Original Contract
Discharge
Breach of Contract
Remedies for Breach of Contract
Dispute Settlement

侵权法 TORTS

Intentional Torts
Defenses to Intentional Torts
Negligence
Cause in Fact
Proximate Cause
Multiple Tortfeasors
Damages for Personal Injuries
Limited Duty: Special Limitations on the Scope of Duty
Premises Liability: Duties of Owners and Occupiers of Land
Defenses
Vicarious Liability
Products Liability

Defamation

The Privacy Torts

Competitive Torts

财产法 PROPERTY LAW

Acquisition of Property

Possessory Estates

Future Interests

Concurrent Estates

Landlord and Tenant

Fixtures

Rights in the Land of Another—Easements, Profits, Covenants, and Servitudes

Conveyancing

Cooperatives, Condominiums, and Zoning

Nuisance

证据法 EVIDENCE LAW

General Considerations

Relevance and Judicial Notice

Real Evidence

Documentary Evidence

Testimonial Evidence

The Hearsay Rule

Procedural Considerations

刑法 / 刑事程序法 CRIMIANL & CRIMINAL PROCEDURE LAW

What Makes a Case a Criminal Case

How to Interpret Criminal Statutes

How Defendants' Mental States Affect Their Responsibility for a Crime

Criminal Offenses

Felonies, Misdemeanors and Infractions

Implications of a Crime's Classification

Constitutional Restrains

Exclusionary Rule

Fourth Amendment

Confessions

Pretrial Procedures

Trial

Guilty Pleas and Plea Bargaining

Constitutional Rights in Relation to Sentence and Punishment

Constitutional Problems on Appeal

Rights during Punishment-probation, Imprisonment, Parole

Double Jeopardy

Forfeiture Actions

知识产权法 INTELLECTUAL PROPERTY LAW

Trade Secrets

Patent

Copyright

Trademark Law

4. WTO 法基础知识

二、法律逻辑推理

三、案例阅读理解分析

四、法律翻译

1. 立法文本翻译

2. 涉外经贸合同翻译

3. 涉外诉讼文书翻译

4. 涉外公证书翻译

5. 判决书翻译

6. 法治新闻报道等综合法律翻译

五、美国法律文书写作

1. 律师信函 legal letters
2. 法律备忘录 law office memos
3. 案件辩论书 briefs

第三部分　考试形式

一、考试形式：计算机考试。考题分主观题和客观题，按考试要求，主客观题一律在计算机上作答。

二、考试时间：上午3个小时，客观题；下午3个小时，主观题。

三、考试评分：总分200分。130分以上，且主、客观两部分得分分别不低于60分为及格标准；170分以上，且主、客观两部分得分分别不低于80分为优秀。

第四部分　考试题型及考核目标

一、单项选择题

法律英语术语；英美法律文化；美国法律基本知识；法律逻辑推理。从A、B、C、D四个选项中选出一个最佳答案。

二、案例阅读

应试者通过快速阅读一篇案例，理解并掌握案例中法律事实（facts）、争议问题（issues）、法律适用（application）、分析推理（analysis）和法庭意见（holding）等。在此基础上，简略回答有关问题或写出案情摘要（case brief）。

三、法律翻译

了解中国法和英美法基本知识及相关法律文化知识。该部分着重考查法律语言的综合表达能力，主要是法律文体片段的中、英文互译。要求应试者有较好的中英文法律语言书面表达能力，了解法律翻译的基本原则和中、英法律语言应用特点。

四、法律写作

要求应试者能正确熟练地撰写涉外律师信函（legal letters）、法律备忘录（law office memos）、案件辩论书（briefs）等。考生应能：（1）做到语法、拼写、标点正确，用词恰当；（2）遵循特定文体格式；（3）合理组织文章结构，使其内容统一、连贯；（4）根据写作目的和特定读者，恰当选用语域。

第五部分　试题结构示例

PART ONE

单项选择题（Multiple Choice Questions）共 100 分
本部分试题由以下四部分内容组成：
1. 法律英语术语及英美法律文化（10%～15%）
2. 美国法律基本知识（70%～75%）
3. WTO 法基本知识（5%～10%）
4. 逻辑推理（5%～10%）

PART TWO

Section I　案例阅读（Case Reading and Comprehension）共 25 分
本部分试题包括一篇真实案例。要求应试者在准确、快速阅读案例后，根据获得的案例中的信息，简略回答有关问题或写出案情摘要（case brief）。

Section II　法律翻译（Legal Translation）共 40 分
本部分试题有两节，A 和 B。A 是中译英，B 是英译中，各占 20 分。

Section III　法律写作（Legal Writing）共 35 分
要求应试者根据题目给出的信息，用英文撰写一封律师函（legal letter），起草意向书（letter of intent）或写一篇法律备忘录（law office memo）；或根据题目所提供的案例，代表某一方写一篇案件辩论书（brief）。

第六部分 考试样题及参考答案

法律英语证书（LEC）全国统一考试样题
Legal English Certificate Test

PART ONE

Multiple Choice Questions: There are four possible answers for each of the following questions. You must choose the best answer to each question under the given cricumstances.

1. Rescission

    A. Cancellation of a contract.

    B. Published decisions of an administrative agency.

    C. The formal rejection of something, typically a belief, claim, or course of action.

    D. The revision of a contract's terms to reflect trade usage or the substitution of one contract party for another.

2. Subpoena

    A. A lower court ruling.

    B. A notice issued by police to ask a suspect to report a crime.

    C. A writ ordering a person to attend a court.

    D. Evidence for the prosecution given by a participant in or an accomplice to the crime being tried.

3. Caveat Emptor

    A. Implied warranty of fitness for use.

    B. Principle to protect consumers from unscrupulous sellers.

    C. Principle that the buyer alone is responsible for checking the quality and suitability of goods before a purchase is made.

    D. Election made by parties to a letter of credit to apply the Uniform

Customs and Practice for Documentary Credits.

4. Public Nuisance

    A. One unreasonably interferes with the use and enjoyment of nearby property.
    B. All criminal offense, consisting of an interference with the rights of the community at large, which may include anything from the obstruction of a highway to public gaming-house or indecent exposure.
    C. Like negligence in that courts weigh and balance a number of factors to decide whether a particular activity constitutes a nuisance.
    D. It interferes with a right of the general public and also interferes with a particular person's use and enjoyment of his land.

5. Sub Judice

    A. Under judicial consideration and therefore prohibited from public discussion elsewhere.
    B. A lease of a property by a tenant to a subtenant.
    C. An agreement between opposing attorneys on any matter relating to the proceedings or trial.
    D. A writ or order to compel attendance in a court with a penalty for failure to do so.

6. Death Sentence

    A. A sentence that imposes the death penalty.
    B. A sentence that gives more punishment than is allowed by law.
    C. A sentence that imprisons the convicted criminal for life.
    D. The highest level of punishment provided by law for a particular crime.

7. Equitable Remedy

    A. A remedy, usu. a nonmonetary one such as an injunction or specific performance, obtained when available legal remedies, usu. monetary damages, cannot adequately redress the injury.

B. A remedy that, under the circumstances, can be pursued expeditiously before the aggrieved party has incurred substantial detriment.

C. A temporary remedy awarded before judgment and pending the action's disposition.

D. A nonjudicial remedy provided by an administrative agency.

8. Voidable

   A. Null and void.

   B. Valid until annulled.

   C. A breach of contract.

   D. Valid.

9. Affirm

   A. To set aside a precedent by expressly deciding that it should no longer be controlling law.

   B. To overturn a judgment on appeal.

   C. To confirm a judgment on appeal.

   D. To abrogate or cancel a contract unilaterally or by agreement.

10. Presumption of Innocence

    A. A legal assumption that a court is required to make if certain facts are established and no contradictory evidence is produced.

    B. A type of rebuttable presumption that may be, but as a matter of law need not be, drawn from another established fact or group of facts.

    C. The fundamental principle that a person may not be convicted of a crime unless the government proves guilt beyond a reasonable doubt, without any burden placed on the accused to prove innocence.

    D. The doctrine that the holder of a patent is entitled to a statutory presumption that the patent is valid and that the burden is on a challenger to prove invalidity.

11. True Bill

    A. The formal process for suing an attorney or officer of the court.

    B. A grand jury's notion that insufficient evidence exists for an indictment on a criminal charge.

    C. A bill in equity to enjoin a judgment and to obtain a new trial because of some fact that would render enforcement of the judgment inequitable.

    D. A grand jury's notion that a criminal charge should go before a petty jury for trial.

12. Double Jeopardy

    A. A plea consisting in two or more distinct grounds of complaint or defense for the same issue.

    B. The fact of being prosecuted or sentenced twice for substantially the same offense.

    C. The punishability of a crime in both the country where a suspect is being held and a country asking for the suspect to be handed over to stand trial.

    D. A set of principles permitting greater opportunity or greater lenience for one class of people than for another, usu. based on a difference such as gender or race.

13. What is the legal department of the federal government called in the United States?

    A. Department of Homeland Security.

    B. State Department.

    C. Department of Justice.

    D. Legal Department.

14. Which of the following is *NOT* true about the United States federal court system?

    A. The United States District Courts are the trial-level courts.

    B. The United States Higher Court is the first level court of appeal.

C. The United States Supreme Court is the final arbiter of the law.

D. The United States federal court system is based on a four-tiered structure.

15. A grants his mother B a right to live in and use A's beachfront house in City until B dies. What kind of interest in the realty does B get?

    A. A life estate.

    B. An easement.

    C. A future interest.

    D. A possessory interest.

16. Requirements of adverse possession are the following EXCEPT

    A. exclusive and actual possession.

    B. open and notorious possession.

    C. hostile and under a claim of right.

    D. interrupted possession for the statutory period.

17. Which of the following is an element of the tort of false imprisonment?

    A. Defendant voluntarily confined the plaintiff to a bounded area.

    B. Defendant negligently confined plaintiff within a bounded area.

    C. Both A and B.

    D. Neither A nor B.

18. Jack is angry at his girlfriend Holly for neglecting him and concentrating on watching TV. While she is visiting, Jack decides to teach her a lesson by locking her in the TV room. Several hours later, he reconsiders and unlocks the door. Unbeknownst to him, however, Holly was sleeping the entire time, and didn't realize she was locked in. Which of the following statements is true?

    A. Holly may not sue Jack for false imprisonment because Jack loves her.

    B. Holly may not sue Jack for false imprisonment because Jack changed his mind and set her free.

C. Holly may not sue Jack for false imprisonment because she was sleeping the entire time.

D. Holly may sue Jack for false imprisonment.

19. A cruise ship with 300 passengers was hit in a big storm and half of its passengers died because it only prepared lifeboats for 150 passengers. When sued, the cruise company presented evidence showing that the custom in the cruise industry is to have lifeboats sufficient for only half of the ship's passengers. Which of the following statements is true?

    A. The cruise company has a complete defense.

    B. The custom in the cruise industry is unreasonable therefore not a defense.

    C. The custom in the cruise industry is conclusive evidence of what the standard of care is.

    D. The cruise company will win the case.

20. Smith owns a shipping business in State A. A criminal statute in State A requires that animals on ships be penned separately to prevent the spread of disease. Smith didn't do so when shipping some dogs for Abraham and pigs for Brown. During a violent rainstorm, all of the pigs were washed overboard. Brown sues Smith claiming that the statutory breach is proof of negligence. Which of the following statements is true?

    A. Smith's violation of the criminal statute is conclusive evidence of negligence.

    B. Since the dogs were not washed overboard, Smith did not commit negligence.

    C. Smith is not liable because the statute was not intended to prevent the pigs from being washing overboard.

    D. Smith is not liable because there was a force majeure event.

21. Larry invited Joan to visit his new house. Joan had a fall in his yard and was injured. When determining whether Larry is liable for Joan's injury,

the court needs to determine Joan's status first. Which of the following statements is *NOT* true?

A. Joan is an invitee.

B. Joan is a social guest.

C. Joan is a licensee.

D. Joan is an invited guest.

Questions 22—23 are based on the following facts:

A Co. sent a letter to B Co. stating that "our company would like to sell Pure Brand bottled water at $20 per case to your company according to your requirements since Jan. 1 next year and throughout the calendar year." B Co. promptly replied, "We agree to have you meet our requirements for Pure Brand bottled water during the coming year, on the terms stated." Then B Co. placed several orders and all were duly delivered. However, on June 1, B Co. received another letter from A Co. asking for increase of the price to $35. B Co. did not agree, and had to buy another brand of bottled water at $30 from C Co. Since profits declined, B Co. sued A Co. for damages.

22. The original agreement between A Co. and B Co. can be best described as

   A. A bilateral contract.

   B. A unilateral contract.

   C. An option contract.

   D. Not an enforceable contract.

23. A Co.'s best defense is_____

   A. The original promise was illusory because no specific quantities were stated.

   B. The agreement between A Co. and B Co. was a series of unilateral contracts, cancelable at will.

   C. Commercial impracticability.

   D. A Co. never made a valid offer to B Co.

Questions 24—26 are based on the following facts:

Bella is a smoker. When she discovered that she was pregnant, she and her husband invited her parents to have dinner together. During the meal, her father told her, "If you will give up smoking until the due date for the baby, I will give you $10,000 at the end of the time." Bella agreed. However, she was not sure whether her father was serious so she asked her mother the following day. Her mother said, "If your father won't pay, I'll give you the money from my own account." So Bella quit smoking that day and never smoked again. Unfortunately, however, on the day the baby was born, Bella's parents were both killed in a car accident.

24. Assuming that Bella sues her father's estate for payment of the money, which of the following statements is true?

   A. Quitting smoking constituted valid consideration.

   B. Bella has not suffered any damage by quitting smoking.

   C. Bella's father has never made an offer.

   D. Bella's mother has never made an offer.

25. Assuming that Bella sues her father's estate for payment of the money, will she prevail?

   A. No, because she will be unable to prove the terms of the oral contract between her and her father since he is dead.

   B. No, because her father's promise to pay was extinguished upon his death.

   C. Yes, because she has performed under a valid contract.

   D. Yes, because she changed her position in reliance on her father's promise.

26. Assuming that Bella sues her mother's estate for the money if her father's estate refuses to pay, what is the best defense for the defendant?

   A. The contract between Bella and her mother was illusory.

   B. Bella has not been damaged by any breach.

C. The contract between Bella and her mother was oral.

D. No valid consideration to support a contract between Bella and her mother.

27. Zack's yard and York's yard are adjacent to each other and Zack has grown three trees along the border line of his property. Later it is discovered that the border line was wrongfully drawn and one of the trees is actually on York's land. If York sues Zack for committing a tort, the most probable cause of action would be

    A. negligence.

    B. trespass on land.

    C. trespass on chattels.

    D. conversion.

28. Zack's yard and York's yard are adjacent to each other and Zack has grown three trees along the border line of his property. Later it is discovered that the border line was wrongfully drawn and one of the trees is actually on York's land. If York sued Zack for committing a tort and the court held for Zack, the most probable reason would be the following but

    A. Zack did not have intent to trespass.

    B. York would like the trees to be there.

    C. York wrongfully occupied the land where the trees are.

    D. Zack did not grow the trees.

29. X wrote a love letter to Y asking Y out for a date. Y posted the letter on the internet. X may sue Y based on

    A. defamation.

    B. appropriation.

    C. intrusion upon seclusion.

    D. public disclosure of private matters.

30. A held a walking stick standing behind B without B's notice and made a gesture to hit B. At this moment, C accidently ran into A and A's walking stick fell on B's head and injured B severely. If B sues A, which would be the most probable cause of action?

   A. Assault.

   B. Battery.

   C. False Imprisonment.

   D. Intentional Infliction of Emotional Distress.

31. A held a walking stick standing behind B without B's notice and made a gesture to hit B. At this moment, C accidently ran into A and A's walking stick fell on B's head and injured B severely. If B sues A for battery and the court holds for B, most probably it would be because

   A. A intended to threaten B.

   B. C intended to strike B.

   C. it was just an accident.

   D. B was injured the day before.

32. Child received a mail which said on the envelope that "you will receive a free watch if you open this envelope." When he did it, he discovered that the letter inside the envelope required him to subscribe a magazine in order to get the free watch. Child's Father sued the magazine. If the court held for the magazine, the most probable reason would be

   A. there is no consideration.

   B. there is no offer.

   C. there is no acceptance.

   D. the matter is too trivial.

33. Owner of Apartment told Patrick that he would like to sell the Apartment to Patrick at $100,000, and Patrick agreed. When Patrick came back with the check, he discovered that Owner had already sold the Apartment to Peil. If Patrick sues Owner for breach of contract and loses, the most

probable reason would be

A. the offer is not valid.

B. the acceptance is not valid.

C. the price is too low.

D. Patrick did not have evidence that Owner agreed to sell the Apartment to him.

34. The local government made a regulation prohibiting all stores from selling fireworks for public safety reasons. "Sell Anything" is a small grocery store and illegally sells fireworks. David bought some fireworks from Sell Anything one day back home. His elder son Sim fired a firework and blew off one of his fingers; while his younger son Sam swallowed a firework and got very sick. David sued the grocery store for Sim's injury. Which of the following is true?

A. Sell Anything will not lose because David voluntarily bought the fireworks.

B. Sell Anything will lose because it illegally sold the fireworks.

C. Sell Anything will not lose because the quality of the fireworks proves to be good.

D. Sell Anything will lose because David was negligence as well.

35. The local government made a regulation prohibiting all stores from selling fireworks for public safety reasons. "Sell Anything" is a small grocery store and illegally sells fireworks. David bought some fireworks from Sell Anything one day back home. His elder son Sim fired a firework and blew off one of his fingers; while his younger son Sam swallowed a firework and got very sick. David sued the grocery store for Sam's injury. Which of the following is true?

A. Sell Anything will not lose because David voluntarily bought the fireworks.

B. Sell Anything will lose because it illegally sold the fireworks.

C. Sell Anything will not lose because they did not expect that Sam would eat the firework.

D. Sell Anything will lose because David was negligence as well.

36. Kid is twelve years old. One day, he drove his father's car out and hit Pedestrian. When Pedestrian sues Kid, what standard do you think the court should apply?

A. The standard for adults.

B. The standard for 12-year-old children.

C. The standard for minors.

D. A reasonable standard.

37. During a murder trial, Prosecutor planned to introduce a knife as evidence. He said to Judge: "Your Honor, Defendant used this knife to kill the victim." Judge sustained the defense lawyer's objection. Why?

A. Prosecutor did not have personal knowledge about the knife.

B. Prosecutor did not have authority to introduce the knife.

C. Defense lawyer is supposed to introduce the knife.

D. Defense lawyer objected timely.

38. During direct examination, Plaintiff's lawyer asks Witness: "What is your opinion?" If the court overrules Defense lawyer's objection, the most probable reason would be

A. Witness is going to make a hearsay statement.

B. Witness is going to make an argumentative statement.

C. Witness is an expert witness.

D. the question is a compounded question.

39. During a murder trial, Prosecutor asks Witness: "What did Defendant say at that moment?" Witness answered: "He said 'I will kill him!'" What should the defense lawyer do?

A. Object on the ground of hearsay.

B. Object on the ground of misleading.

C. Object on the ground of argumentative.

D. Object and request the court to strike the answer.

40. During a murder trial, Prosecutor asks Witness: "What did Defendant say at that moment?" Defense lawyer objected. What will be the most probable result?

   A. The court will sustain the objection on the ground of hearsay.

   B. The court will sustain the objection on the ground of asked and answered.

   C. The court will overrule the objection because Witness is a minor.

   D. The court will overrule the objection because Prosecutor is direct-examining the Witness.

41. During a murder trial, Prosecutor asks Witness: "What did you hear at that moment?" Defense lawyer objected on the ground of hearsay. If the court overruled the objection, the most probable reasons include the following but

   A. Witness' answer would be used to prove that Witness got notice of the accident.

   B. Witness' answer would be "A bang"!

   C. Witness' answer would show his state of mind.

   D. None of the above.

42. A sues B for breach of contract and asks for $10,000's damages. The court held for A, and granted $5,000 damages. Neither A nor B is satisfied. Who may appeal?

   A. A may appeal.

   B. B may appeal.

   C. Both A and B may appeal.

   D. Neither A nor B may appeal.

43. The court is trying a case with a jury. When the court hearing is almost finished, one of the jurors is seriously sick and cannot stay on the panel.

In order to speed up the trial proceeding, the judge selects another person as a juror, and tells him everything about the case that is being tried, and then let him sit in with the other jurors to make a verdict. Which of the following statements is *NOT* true?

A. It is not appropriate and the case must be retried.

B. It is appropriate because the person selected is an alternate juror.

C. It is not appropriate because the new person did not have a chance to develop his own thoughts.

D. It is appropriate because the judge has already told the new person about everything relating to the trial.

44. In the United States, if both federal court and state court have jurisdiction over a case, which of the following statements is true?

    A. The courts may discuss and decide which court should try this case.

    B. Plaintiff may decide whether go to the federal court or the state court.

    C. Defendant may decide whether go to the federal court or the state court.

    D. Plaintiff may make the first choice; if Plaintiff chooses to go to a state court, Defendant may move to remove the case to the federal court.

45. Which of the following statements about the jury system is *NOT* true?

    A. Jury system has already been abolished in common law countries.

    B. To have a jury trial is a constitutional right of US citizens.

    C. Any defendant in a criminal case has the right to a jury trial.

    D. In a civil case, the parties may waive their right to a jury trial upon consultation.

46. A sues B for personal injury. The trial court granted $10,000 actual damages and $5,000 punitive damages. B appealed to the appellate court challenging the actual damages, but the appellate court affirmed. B then appealed to the supreme court of the state based on the ground that the punitive damages was wrongfully granted. What would be the most

probable result?

A. The supreme court will consider this argument seriously.

B. The supreme court will not consider this argument at all.

C. The supreme court will send this case back to the appellate court.

D. The supreme court will send this case back to the trial court.

47. Which of the following is *NOT* a subject of intellectual property law?

A. Ownership of a trademark.

B. Ownership of copyright.

C. Ownership of a patent.

D. Ownership of Real property.

48. In order to determine whether or not a particular use is a fair use, which of the following factors does *NOT* need to be analyzed?

A. Purpose and character of the use.

B. Nature of the copyrighted work.

C. Amount and substantiality taken.

D. Negative comments contained.

49. An artistic ornamental design could be the subject matter for patent, trademark or copyright protection, but

A. it may not be protected under all three at the same time.

B. it may not be protected as a trademark if it has registered as a copyrightable work of art.

C. it may not be protected as a design patent, and a trademark or a copyrightable work.

D. it may not be protected as a copyrightable work, and a trademark or design patent.

50. "Originality" in a copyrighted work means minimum creativity; thus it would not rise to that level if the work is

A. a telephone directory since compilation of raw facts does not involve any original efforts.

B. a news story since everyone may write about it.

C. created by using the name of a famous author without permission.

D. a movie adapted from a novel of another author under permission.

51. Under the trademark law, any unauthorized use of another's mark would constitute trademark infringement. Therefore a prima facie case is established when

　　A. a trader uses an APPLE® computer packaging box and puts his own computer in it for sale.

　　B. a book publisher publishes a children's book in which all of the cartoon characters are registered trademarks owned by another publisher.

　　C. a computer store puts up a sign that reads: "IBM, APPLE and DELL Dealer" without authorization from any of the big names.

　　D. a used computer shop buys old IBM®, APPLE® and DELL® computers and resells them to customers at a bargain.

52. The trademark registration requires a mark be distinctive, i.e., the closer in meaning to the underlying product, the weaker of the mark for protection. Thus a trademark would be considered as

　　A. generic as in GREY HOUND for long distance bus service.

　　B. descriptive as in APPLE for a computer product.

　　C. suggestive as in STACCATO for Italian women's high heel shoes.

　　D. arbitrary or fanciful as in ASPIRIN for a pain relief medicine.

53. A trade secret is the technology or know-how which can bring economic benefit to its owner, for as long as the technology or know-how remains a secret, disclosure of which is not proper through unfair methods of competition. Which one of the following is generally considered as unfair competition?

　　A. By studying the publicly available product to find out the "secret".

　　B. By consulting a highly renowned professor who owns many patents similar in the technology.

C. By offering attractive salaries to an engineer working on the technology or know-how of its owner.

D. By one's own research and innovative development of the same or separate technology or know-how.

54. E, who was sent to prison for nine years for car theft, vowed to get even with C, the prosecutor at his trial. While in prison, E was told by another prisoner, D, that when C was in private practice as a criminal defense attorney, he had represented D in a drug charge. D claimed that because he did not have the cash to pay C his fees, he offered to pay his fees with five ounces of cocaine, and C accepted.

    Although E had no independent reason to believe that what D said was true, when he got out of prison he learned that C was running for District Attorney. E went to one of the local papers and sold them the story for $1,000. In the article that resulted, E was quoted as saying "I only hope that C suffers like I had to suffer for the last nine years."

    As a result of this article, C withdrew from the race, and although the applicable statute of limitation for any criminal statute had run, C was disbarred for moral unfitness. In a suit by C against E for defamation of character, the probable result would be

    A. C prevails because E acted with deliberate malice towards C.

    B. C prevails if the story was false.

    C. E prevails because the story was newsworthy.

    D. E prevails if he honestly believed the truth of the assertion made by D.

55. A statute in a jurisdiction makes it a crime to sell ammunition to a minor (defined as a person under the age of 18). The courts have interpreted this statute as creating a strict liability offense that does not require knowledge of the age of the purchaser and as creating vicarious liability. Duncan, who was 16 years old, but looked four or five years older, entered a store owned by Mathews and asked a clerk for a box of .22 caliber shells. Mathews had instructed her employees not to sell ammunition to minors.

The clerk asked Duncan his age. Duncan said he was 20. The clerk then placed a box of shells on the counter and asked, "Anything else?" Duncan said that was all he wanted but then discovered he did not have enough money to pay for the shells, so the clerk put the box back onto the shelf.

If Mathews, the owner of the store, is charged with attempting to violate the statute, her best argument would be that

  A. it was impossible for the sale to have occurred.

  B. she had strictly instructed her employees not to sell ammunition to minors.

  C. Duncan lied about his age.

  D. the clerk did not have the mental state needed for attempt.

56. Technix, Inc. produces the most up-to-date, high-speed computers on the market, and Cruncher Corporation is on the cutting edge of electronics technology. Cruncher and Technix contracted to purchase/sell a "Yellow Giant" computer. The written contract stated that Cruncher would purchase "one Technix 'Yellow Giant' computer at a price of $175,000." At the time, the going price for Yellow Giant computers was $150,000. When Technix delivered a Yellow Giant on the specified date, Cruncher refused to accept delivery and refused to pay. Technix sued Cruncher for breach, claiming that its expensive computers were manufactured to order and so it was forced to dispose of the Yellow Giant at a price far below fair market value. In defending the suit, Cruncher's president wished to testify that Cruncher rejected the Yellow Giant because both parties knew that Cruncher really wanted a "Purple Giant," a machine much faster than the Yellow Giant, but which the parties agreed would be called in the contract a "Yellow Giant" to keep competitors in the dark as to Cruncher's new capabilities, and that the parties had executed contracts in the past that had specified a less powerful computer than the model that was actually delivered.

Should the testimony of Cruncher's president be admitted?

  A. Yes, because Cruncher is entitled to reformation of the contract.

B. Yes, because the president's testimony would explain the meaning of a disputed contract term.

C. No, because the parole evidence rule applies and the president's testimony contradicts a term in the written contract.

D. No, because the Statute of Frauds applies because the contract is for a large amount of money.

Questions 57—58 are based on the following fact situation:

The state of F has recently had a problem with people dealing in, and with, its booming garment industry. The use of independent contractors by major garment makers had led to the hiring of illegal aliens to work under conditions reminiscent of 19th century sweatshops.

The legislature of F enacted a statute to remedy the situation and to protect its citizens against the problems in the future. The statute provides

I. That all garment makers must be licensed by the state attorney general.

II. That all subcontractors (defined separately in the statue) must be separately licensed by the attorney general and must have been a citizen of the United States for five years and a resident of F for one year.

57. The requirement that garment makers be licensed by the attorney general is

A. constitutional, because it is within the proper scope of the exercise of the police powers of the state.

B. constitutional, because the attorney general is designated as the proper person to enforce the law.

C. unconstitutional, as a burden on interstate commerce.

D. unconstitutional, as a violation of the Privileges and Immunities Clause of the Fourteenth Amendment.

58. The second clause of the legislation concerning subcontractors is subject to a constitutional challenge based on

A. the Equal Protection Clause of the Fourteenth Amendment.

B. the Privileges and Immunities Clause of the Fourteenth Amendment.

C. the Due Process Clause of the Fifth Amendment.

D. the Tenth Amendment reserved powers of the state.

59. In litigation over the estate of Baggs, who died intestate, Payton, who is 18 years old, claimed to be Baggs's niece and entitled, therefore, to a share of his large estate. In support of her claim, Payton offered in evidence a Bible, properly identified as having belonged to Baggs's family, in the front of which was a list of family births, marriages, and deaths. The list recorded Payton's birth to Baggs's oldest sister.

To prove that Payton is Baggs's niece, the Bible listing is

A. admissible as an ancient document.

B. admissible as a family record.

C. inadmissible, because it is hearsay not within any exception.

D. inadmissible, because there was no showing of firsthand knowledge by the one who wrote it.

60. Taylor and Scott, an unmarried couple, purchased a condominium as tenants in common and lived in the condominium for three years. Subsequently, they made an oral agreement that, on the death of either of them, the survivor would own the entire condominium, and, as a result, they decided they did not need wills.

Two years later, Taylor and Scott were involved in the same automobile accident. Taylor was killed immediately. Scott died one week later. Both died intestate. Taylor's sole heir is his brother, Mark. Scott's sole heir is her mother, Martha. Mark claimed one-half of the condominium, and Martha claimed all of it. The jurisdiction has no applicable statute except for the Statute of Frauds; nor does it recognize common law marriage.

In an appropriate action by Martha claiming the entire ownership of the condominium, the court will find that

A. Martha owns the entire interest because Taylor and Scott did not make wills in reliance upon their oral agreement.

B. Martha owns the entire interest because she is entitled to reformation of the deed to reflect the oral agreement.

C. Mark and Martha each own an undivided one-half interest because Taylor and Scott each died as the result of the same accident.

D. Mark and Martha each own an undivided one-half interest because the Statute of Frauds applies.

61. A state statute provides that only citizens of the United States may be employed by that state. In an action brought in a federal court, a resident alien who was prevented from obtaining state employment as a garbage collector solely because of his alien status challenged the statute's constitutionality as applied to his circumstances.

    Which of the following statements concerning the burden of persuasion applicable to this suit is correct?

    A. The alien must demonstrate that there is no rational relationship between the citizenship requirement and any legitimate state interest.

    B. The alien must demonstrate that the citizenship requirement is not necessary to advance an important state interest.

    C. The state must demonstrate that there is a rational relationship between the citizenship requirement and a legitimate state interest.

    D. The state must demonstrate that the citizenship requirement is necessary to advance a compelling state interest.

62. Chemco designed and built a large tank on its premises for the purpose of storing highly toxic gas. The tank developed a sudden leak and escaping toxic gas drifted into the adjacent premises, where Nyman lived. Nyman inhaled the gas and died as a result.

    In a suit brought by Nyman's personal representative against Chemco, which of the following must be established if the claim is to prevail?

    I. The toxic gas that escaped from Chemco's premises was the cause of Nyman's death.

    II. The tank was built in a defective manner.

III. Chemco was negligent in designing the tank.

A. I. only.

B. I. and II. only.

C. I. and III. only.

D. I., II., and III.

63. Pullen used aluminum brackets in her business. On the telephone listed as hers in the telephone book, Pullen received a call in which the caller said, "This is John Denison of Denison Hardware Company. We have a special on aluminum brackets this week at 30% off." Pullen ordered brackets from the caller. When the brackets were never delivered, Pullen sued Denison for breach of contract.

At trial, Denison, who denies having made the telephone call, objects to Pullen's testimony concerning it. When asked, Pullen testifies that, aside from the telephone call, she had never heard Denison speak until she met him in the judge's chambers before the trial and that, in her opinion, the voice on the telephone was Denison's.

The strongest argument for admission of Pullen's testimony concerning the telephone call is that

A. the call related to business reasonably transacted over the telephone.

B. the call was received at a number assigned to Pullen by the telephone company.

C. after hearing Denison speak in chambers, Pullen recognized Denison's voice as that of the person on the telephone.

D. self-identification is sufficient authentication of a telephone call.

64. Drake owned a small warehouse that he leased to Teague, who used it as a storage and distribution center for fresh cut flowers being shipped to area florists. Drake wanted to put Teague out of business so that he could lease the warehouse to someone else at a higher rent. He entered the warehouse one night using a master key, and turned off the cooling system to destroy the flowers. To ensure that all of Teague's inventory would be destroyed,

he also deployed several kerosene space heaters. While he was filling one, a small amount of kerosene spilled and was ignited by an ash from his cigarette. Although the fire that started was small at first, Drake panicked when he saw the flames and ran out of the building. The fire eventually spread to the walls of the building and heavily damaged it before being extinguished by firefighters.

If Drake is charged with arson, can he be found guilty?

A. Yes, because Drake caused the fire during the commission of a malicious felony.

B. Yes, because Drake did nothing when the kerosene caught on fire.

C. No, because Drake did not intend to start the building on fire.

D. No, because Drake cannot be liable for arson of a building that he owned.

65. Dietz and Atkins worked together as pickpockets. Dietz approached Verner from the front to distract him, holding a small camera and asking him to take a picture, while Atkins came up from behind with a knife to slice open Verner's back pocket of his pants and remove his wallet. Verner was drunk and believed Dietz had a gun and was trying to rob him, but was unaware of Atkins behind him. Verner reached into his back pocket to hand over his wallet and was cut by Atkins's knife as it was slicing through his pocket. The wallet dropped to the ground as Verner clutched his hand. Atkins picked it up and Dietz and Atkins fled while Verner knelt on the ground in pain. Dietz was apprehended shortly thereafter and charged with robbery. Should Dietz be found guilty?

A. Yes, because Atkins obtained the property by means of force.

B. Yes, because Verner believed that Dietz would shoot him if he did not give up his wallet.

C. No, because neither Dietz nor Atkins intended to use force against Verner to obtain the property.

D. No, because Verner's belief that Dietz was robbing him was unreasonable.

66. Professor Peterson, an expert on American Colonial and Revolutionary History, conducted full-day tours through the historic sites of Philadelphia every Wednesday and Thursday through the summer months. Peterson's fee for his services was $105, which did not include the entrance fees for several of the historic sites. Other persons and organizations conducted various American history tours through the city for somewhat less than Peterson, but Peterson's tour was generally rated the best by the leading tourist guidebooks because Peterson personally conducted the tours and shared his encyclopedic knowledge of American history and the city of Philadelphia.

David had recently moved to Philadelphia, and all of his co-workers praised Professor Peterson's tour, but David was not inclined to pay $105 for a tour of the historic sites of his new city. Therefore, David took a day off one Thursday and "hung around" the Liberty Bell monument, where Peterson's tour started. That day Peterson was conducting 27 persons on the tour. Most of the participants had paid in advance, but Peterson was holding up a sign with information about the tour and handing out brochures, one of which David took. Peterson accepted a few additional participants who signed up on the spot, but David was not among them. All day long, David hung around at the fringe of this group, paying the entrance fees separately but following the group through different historic sites. However, he always positioned himself close enough to Peterson's group so that he could hear virtually every word of Peterson's lecture, although David did not ask the Professor any questions. David signed his name and address on the register at Independence Hall. Peterson noted this and took down the information. Two days after the tour concluded, David received a bill from Peterson in the amount of $105. David will most likely be required to pay Peterson

A. $105, because that is the contract price for the tour.

B. $105, because the amount of the contract was less than $500, making the Statute of Frauds inapplicable.

C. $105, if that is a reasonable fee for the lectures based on Peterson's expertise.

D. nothing, because the historical sited were open to the public and David paid his own way.

67. In compliance with a federal statute requiring buildings to be made accessible to persons with disabilities, Walter installed wheelchair ramps at both entrances to his office building located on Blackacre, which he had owned for many years. One year later, Walter entered into a contract with Barbara to sell Blackacre, including the office building. After having the property surveyed, Barbara notified Walter that she was not going to complete the sale because the wheelchair ramp on the south side of the building extended over the property line and into the adjoining parcel of Whiteacre, making the title unmarketable. Walter insisted that Barbara proceed with the sale, and brought an action to compel her performance.

If the court were to find that title is marketable, it will be because

A. the wheelchair ramp is required by federal law.

B. Walter currently owns Whiteacre and acquired Whiteacre and Blackacre as part of larger parcel.

C. the wheelchair ramp extends only 10 inches over the property line.

D. the contract between Walter and Barbara requires Walter to convey only a quitclaim deed.

68. An ordinance of City makes it unlawful to park a motor vehicle on a City street within 10 feet of a fire hydrant. At 1:55 p.m. Parker, realizing he must be in Bank before it closed at 2 p.m. and finding no other space available, parked his automobile in front of a fire hydrant on a City street. Parker then hurried into the Bank, leaving his aged neighbor, Ned, as a passenger in the rear seat of the car. About five minutes later, and while Parker was still in Bank, Driver was driving down the street. Driver swerved to avoid what he mistakenly thought was a hole in the street and sideswiped Parker's car. Parker's car was turned over on top of the

hydrant, breaking the hydrant and causing a small flood of water. Parker's car was severely damaged and Ned was badly injured. There is no applicable guest statute and jurisdiction follows traditional contributory negligence rules. If Ned asserts a claim against Parker, the most likely result is that Ned will

A. recover, because Parker's action was negligence per se.

B. recover, because Parker's action was a continuing wrong that contributed to Ned's injuries.

C. not recover, because a reasonably prudent person could not foresee injury to Ned as a result of Parker's action.

D. not recover, because a violation of a city ordinance does not give rise to a civil cause of action.

Questions 69—71 are based on the following fact situation:

On May 1, O telegraphed B, "Will sell you any or all of the lots in Grove subdivision at $5,000 each. Details follow in letter." The letter contained all the necessary details concerning terms of payment, insurance, mortgages, etc., and provided, "This offer remains open until June 1." On May 2, after he had received the telegram but before he had received the letter, B telegraphed O, "Accept your offer with respect to lot 101." Both parties knew that there were 50 lots in the Grove subdivision and that they were numbered 101 through 150.

69. For this question only, assume that O and B were bound by a contract for the sale of lot 101 for $5,000, that on May 3 O telephoned B and stated that because he had just discovered that a shopping center was going to be erected adjacent to the Grove subdivision, he would "need to have $6,000 for each of the lots including lot 101," that B thereupon agreed to pay him $6,000 for lot 101, and that on May 6, B telegraphed, "Accept your offer with respect to the rest of the lots," Assuming that two contracts were formed and that there is no controlling statute, B will most

likely be required to pay

A. only $5,000 for each of the 50 lots.

B. only $5,000 for lot 101, but $6,000 for the remaining 49 lots.

C. $6,000 for each of the 50 lots.

D. $6,000 for lot 101, but only $5,000 for the retaining 49 lots.

70. For this question only, assume that on May 5, O telephoned B stating that he had sold lots 102 through 150 to someone else on May 4, and that B thereafter telegraphed O, "Will take the rest of the lots." Assume further that there is no controlling statute. In an action by B against O for breach of contract, B will probably

A. succeed, because O had promised him that the offer would remain open until June 1.

B. succeed, because O's attempted revocation was by telephone.

C. not succeed, because B's power of acceptance was terminated by O's sale of the lots to another party.

D. not succeed, because B's power of acceptance was terminated by effective revocation.

71. For this question only, assume that on May 6, B telegraphed O, "Will take the rest of the lots," and that on May 8, O discovered that he did not have good title to the remaining lots. Which of the following would provide the best legal support to O's contention that he was not liable for breach of contract as to the remaining 49 lots?

A. Impossibility of performance.

B. Unilateral mistake as to basic assumption.

C. Termination of the offer by B's having first contracted to buy lot 101.

D. Excuse by failure of an implied condition precedent.

72. L was the high priest of a small cult of Satan worshippers living in New Arcadia. As a part of the practice of their religious beliefs, a cat was required to be sacrificed to the glory of Satan after a live dissection of the

animal in which it endured frightful pain. In the course of such a religious sacrifice, L was arrested on the complaint of the local Humane Society and charged under a statute punishing cruelty to animals.

On appeal, a conviction of L probably will be

A. sustained, on the grounds that belief in or worship of Satan does not enjoy constitutional protection.

B. sustained, on the grounds that sincere religious belief is not an adequate defense on these facts.

C. overturned, on the grounds that the constitutionally guaranteed freedom of religion and its expression was violated.

D. overturned, on the grounds that the beliefs of the cult members in the need for the sacrifice might be reasonable, and their act was religious.

73. Peters sued Dietrich, claiming that they had entered into an oral agreement whereby Dietrich agreed to hire Peters as Chief Engineer of Dietrich Products and Peters agreed to take the job at a specified salary, and that Dietrich had subsequently breached their employment contract by refusing to hire Peters. At the trial of Peters' suit, Dietrich took the stand and denied having any contract with Peters for employment or otherwise. In response, Peters offers into evidence a properly authenticated phone message to Dietrich's wife, Wanda, that Dietrich had left with the switchboard operator at her office. The message stated, "I know you won't be happy, but I've offered Peters the Chief Engineer position and he's accepted." Dietrich's attorney objects.

The phone message should be ruled

A. admissible, because it is the statement of a party-opponent.

B. admissible, if it is a recent perception.

C. inadmissible, because it is a privileged communication between husband and wife.

D. inadmissible, because it is hearsay not within any recognized exception to the hearsay rule.

Questions 74—75 are based on the following fact situation:

H and W were going through a nasty divorce. W hired P, a private investigator, to spy on H. P followed H to Hotel, where he saw H meet a woman and check into a room. P checked into the adjoining room, placed an illegal listening device on the wall, and listened to the activities of H and the woman in the next room. While P was listening, a burglar broke into P's room and hit P over the head with a blackjack. As a result, P was hospitalized. A state statute sets minimum standards for hotel room locks, and Hotel has complied with the statute. Another statute makes adultery a crime.

74. If P sues Hotel for his injuries

　　A. P will prevail if Hotel's management had reason to believe the locks were inadequate.

　　B. P will prevail, because innkeepers are strictly liable for injuries to their guests from third persons.

　　C. Hotel will prevail, because the burglar was a superseding intervening cause.

　　D. Hotel will prevail, because it was in compliance with the state statute regarding locks.

75. If H sues P for invasion of privacy

　　A. H will win, because he had an expectation of privacy in his hotel room.

　　B. H will win, because P's electronic eavesdropping was illegal.

　　C. H will lose, because adultery is illegal.

　　D. H will lose if P published nothing about H's activities.

76. In 1965, Hubert Green executed his will which in pertinent part provided, "I hereby give, devise, and bequeath Greenvale to my surviving widow for life, remainder to such of my children as shall live to attain the age of 30 years, but if any child dies under the age of 30 years survived by a child or children, such child or children shall take and receive the share

which his, her, or their parent would have received had such parent lived to attain the age of 30 years."

At the date of writing his will, Green was married to Susan, and they had two children, Allan and Beth. Susan died in 1970 and Hubert married Waverly in 1972. At his death in 1980, Green was survived by his wife, Waverly, and three children, Allan, Beth, and Carter. Carter, who was born in 1974, was his child by Waverly.

In a jurisdiction that recognizes the common law Rule Against Perpetuities unmodified by statute, the result of the application of the Rule is that the

A. remainder to the children and to the grandchildren is void because Green could have subsequently married a person who was unborn at the time Green executed his will.

B. remainder to the children is valid, but the substitutionary gift to the grandchildren is void because Green could have subsequently married a person who was unborn at the time Green executed his will.

C. gift in remainder to Allan and Beth or their children is valid, but the gift to Carter or his children is void.

D. remainder to the children and the substitutionary gift to the grandchildren are valid.

77. Downs was indicted in state court for bribing a public official. During the course of the investigation, police had demanded and received from Downs's bank the records of Downs's checking account for the preceding two years. The records contained incriminating evidence.

On the basis of a claim of violation of his constitutional rights, Downs moves to prevent the introduction of the records in evidence. His motion should be

A. granted, because a search warrant should have been secured for seizure of the records.

B. granted, because the records covered such an extensive period of time that their seizure unreasonably invaded Downs's right of privacy.

C. denied, because the potential destructibility of the records, coupled with the public interest in proper enforcement of the criminal laws, created an exigent situation justifying the seizure.

D. denied, because the records were business records of the bank in which Downs had no legitimate expectation of privacy.

78. Plummer, a well-known politician, was scheduled to address a large crowd at a political dinner. Just as Plummer was about to sit down at the head table, Devon pushed Plummer's chair to one side. As a result, Plummer fell to the floor. Plummer was embarrassed at being made to look foolish before a large audience but suffered no physical harm.

    If Plummer asserts a claim against Devon for damages because of his embarrassment, will Plummer prevail?

    A. Yes, if Devon knew that Plummer was about to sit on the chair.

    B. Yes, if Devon negligently failed to notice that Plummer was about to sit on the chair.

    C. No, because Plummer suffered no physical harm along with his embarrassment.

    D. No, if in moving the chair Devon intended only a good-natured practical joke on Plummer.

79. Paulsen sued Daly for nonpayment of a personal loan to Daly, as evidenced by Daly's promissory note to Paulsen. Paulsen called Walters to testify that he knows Daly's handwriting and that the signature on the note is Daly's. On direct examination, to identify himself, Walters gave his name and address and testified that he had been employed by a roofing company for seven years.

    During presentation of Daly's case, Daly called Wilson to testify that she is the roofing company's personnel manager and that she had determined, by examining the company's employment records, that Walters had worked there for only three years.

The trial judge should rule that Wilson's testimony is

A. inadmissible, because it is not the best evidence.

B. inadmissible, because it is impeachment on a collateral question.

C. admissible as evidence of a regularly conducted activity.

D. admissible as tending to impeach Walters's credibility.

80. A federal statute set up a program of dental education. The statute provided that the Secretary of Health and Human Services "shall, on a current basis, spend all of the money appropriated for this purpose" and "shall distribute the appropriated funds" by a specified formula to state health departments that agree to participate in the program. In the current year Congress appropriated $100 million for expenditure on this program. To ensure a budget surplus in the current fiscal year, the President issued an executive order directing the various Cabinet Secretaries to cut expenditures in this year by 10% in all categories. He also ordered certain programs to be cut more drastically because he believed that "they are not as important to the general welfare as other programs." The President identified the dental education program as such a program and ordered it to be cut by 50%. Assume that no other federal statutes are relevant.

To satisfy constitutional requirements, how much money must the Secretary of Health and Human Services distribute for the dental education program this year?

A. $50 million, because the President could reasonably determine that this program is not as important to the general welfare as other programs.

B. $50 million, because as chief executive the President has the constitutional authority to control the actions of all of his subordinates by executive order.

C. $90 million, because any more drastic cut for the program would be a denial of equal protection to beneficiaries of this program as compared to beneficiaries of other programs.

D. $100 million, because the President may not unilaterally suspend the effect of a valid federal statute imposing a duty to spend appropriated monies.

81. Four years ago, Owen held Blackacre, a tract of land, in fee simple absolute. In that year he executed and delivered to Price a quitclaim deed which purported to release and quitclaim to Price all of the right, title, and interest of Owen in Blackacre. Price accepted the quitclaim and placed the deed in his safe deposit box.

Owen was indebted to Crider in the amount of $35,000. In September of the current year, Owen executed and delivered to Crider a warranty deed, purporting to convey the fee simple to Blackacre, in exchange for a full release of the debt he owed to Crider. Crider immediately recorded his deed.

In December, Price caused his quitclaim deed to Blackacre to be recorded and notified Crider that he (Price) claimed title.

Assume that there is no evidence of occupancy of Blackacre and assume, further, that the jurisdiction where Blackacre is situated has a recording statute which required good faith and value as elements of the junior claimant's priority. Which of the following is the best comment concerning the conflicting claims of Price and Crider?

A. Price cannot succeed, because the quitclaim deed through which he claims prevents him from being bona fide (in good faith).

B. The outcome will turn on the view taken as to whether Crider paid value within the meaning of the statute requiring this element.

C. The outcome will turn on whether Price paid value (a fact not given in the statement).

D. Price's failure to record until December of the current year stops him from asserting title against Crider.

82. Brown contended that Green owed him $6,000. Green denied that he owed Brown anything. Tired of the dispute, Green eventually signed a

promissory note by which he promised to pay Brown $5,000 in settlement of their dispute.

In an action by Brown against Green on the promissory note, which of the following, if true, would afford Green the best defense?

A. Although Brown honestly believed that $6,000 was owed by Green, Green knew that it was not owed.

B. Although Brown knew that the debt was not owed, Green honestly was in doubt whether it was owed.

C. The original claim was based on an oral agreement, which the Statute of Frauds required to be in writing.

D. The original claim was an action on a contract, which was barred by the applicable statute of limitations.

83. Ellis, an electrical engineer, designed an electronic game known as Zappo. Ellis entered into a licensing agreement with Toyco under which Toyco agreed to manufacture Zappo according to Ellis's specifications and to market it and pay a royalty to Ellis.

Carla, whose parents had purchased a Zappo game for her, was injured while playing with the game. Carla recovered a judgment against Toyco on the basis of a finding that the Zappo game was defective because of Ellis's improper design.

In a claim for indemnity against Ellis, will Toyco prevail?

A. Yes, because as between Ellis and Toyco, Ellis was responsible for the design of Zappo.

B. Yes, because Toyco and Ellis were joint tortfeasors.

C. No, because Toyco, as the manufacturer, was strictly liable to Carla.

D. No, if Toyco, by a reasonable inspection, could have discovered the defect in the design of Zappo.

84. Defendant was charged with murder. His principal defense was that he had killed in hot blood and should be guilty only of manslaughter. The judge instructed the jury that the state must prove guilt beyond a

reasonable doubt, that the killing was presumed to be murder, and that the charge could be reduced to manslaughter, and Defendant accordingly found guilty of this lesser offense, if Defendant showed by a fair preponderance of the evidence that the killing was committed in the heat of passion on sudden provocation. Defendant was convicted of murder. On appeal, he seeks a new trial and claims error in the judge's instructions to the jury. Defendant's conviction will most probably be

A. affirmed, because the judge carefully advised the jury of the state's obligation to prove guilt beyond a reasonable doubt.

B. affirmed, because Defendant's burden to show hot blood was not one of ultimate persuasion but only one of producing evidence to rebut a legitimate presumption.

C. reversed, because the instruction put a burden on Defendant that denied him due process of law.

D. reversed, because presumptions have a highly prejudicial effect and thus cannot be used on behalf of the state in a criminal case.

85. While on walking patrol in a commercial district in the early evening, Officer Murdoch noticed that a light was on in Walker's Machine Shop. Curious about what was going on inside, the officer tried to look through the window of the shop, but it had been painted on the inside so that only a strip about three inches at the top, eight feet above street level, was still transparent. Officer Murdoch quietly brought two trash cans from a neighboring business over to the window, stood on them and saw, through the strip of unpainted window, that the shop owner's son Tommy was inside with a friend, sucking white powder into his nose through a rolled up tube of paper from off a small mirror. Recognizing from his experience and training that Tommy was snorting cocaine, Officer Murdoch knocked at the front door to the shop, and Tommy let him in. Murdoch immediately arrested Tommy and his friend. In the back room of the shop through whose window he had peered, Murdoch found and

seized several grams of cocaine, a razor blade, and a mirror.

In Tommy's subsequent prosecution for possession of cocaine, Tommy seeks to bar introduction of the cocaine, mirror, and razor blade into evidence. His motion will probably be

A. granted, because Officer Murdoch could not have known that Tommy was snorting cocaine absent a chemical test of the substance being snorted.

B. granted, because Officer Murdoch violated Tommy's reasonable expectation of privacy.

C. denied, because the search was incident to a valid arrest.

D. denied, because Tommy consented to Officer Murdoch's entry into the shop.

86. Parmott sued Dexter in an automobile collision case. At trial, Parmott wishes to show by extrinsic evidence that Wade, Dexter's primary witness, is Dexter's partner in a gambling operation. This evidence is

A. admissible as evidence of Wade's character.

B. admissible as evidence of Wade's possible bias in favor of Dexter.

C. inadmissible, because criminal conduct can be shown only by admission or record of conviction.

D. inadmissible, because bias must be shown on cross-examination and not by extrinsic evidence.

Questions 87—89 are based on the following fact situation:

F had made a legally binding promise to furnish his son Junior and the latter's fiancee a house on their wedding day, planned for June 10 of the following year. Pursuant to that promise, F telephoned his old contractor—friend S and made the following oral agreement—each making full and accurate written notes thereof:

S was to cut 30 trees into fireplace logs from a specified portion of a certain one-acre plot owned by F, and F was to pay therefore $20 per tree. S agreed further to build a house on the plot conforming to the specifications of Plan OP5 published by Builders, Inc. for a construction price of $18,000. F agreed to make payments of $2,000 on the first of every month for nine months beginning August 1 upon monthly presentation of a certificate by Builders, Inc. that the specifications of Plan OP5 were being met.

S delivered the cut logs to F in July, when he also began building the house. F made three $2,000 payments for the work done in July, August, and September, without requiring a certificate. S worked through October, but no work was done from November 1 to the end of February because of bad weather; and F made no payments during that period. S did not object. On March 1, S demanded payment of $2,000; but F refused on the grounds that no construction work had been done for four months and Builders had issued no certificate. S thereupon abandoned work and repudiated the agreement.

87. Assuming that S committed a total breach on March 1, what would be the probable measure of F's damages in an action against S for breach of contract?

   A. Restitution of the three monthly installments paid in August, September, and October.

   B. What it would cost to get the house completed by another contractor, minus installments not yet paid to S.

   C. The difference between the market value of the partly built house, as of the time of S's breach, and the market value of the house if completed according to specifications.

   D. In addition to other legally allowable damages, an allowance for F's mental distress if the house cannot be completed in time for Junior's wedding on June 10.

88. Assuming that S committed a total breach on March 1, and assuming further that he was aware when the agreement was made of the purpose for which F wanted the completed house, which of the following, if true, would best support F's claim for consequential damages on account of

delay beyond June 10 in getting the house finished?

A. Junior and his bride, married on June 10, would have to pay storage charges on their wedding gifts and new furniture until the house could be completed.

B. Junior's fiancee jilted Junior on June 10 and ran off with another man who had a new house.

C. F was put to additional expense in providing Junior and his bride, married on June 10, with temporary housing.

D. On June 10, F paid a $5,000 judgment obtained against him in a suit filed March 15 by an adjoining landowner on account of F's negligent excavation, including blasting, in an attempt to finish the house himself after S's repudiation.

89. What was the probable legal effect of the following?

I. S's failure to object to F's making no payments on November 1, December 1, January 1, and February1.

II. F's making payments in August through October without requiring a certificate from Builders'.

A. Estoppel-type waiver as to both I. and II.

B. Waiver of delay in payment as to I. and revocable waiver as to II.

C. Mutual rescission of the contract by I. combined with II.

D. Discharge of F's duty to make the four payments as to I. and estoppel-type waiver as to II.

90. Rogers gave Mitchell a power of attorney containing the following provision: "My attorney, Mitchell, is specifically authorized to sell and convey any part or all of my real property".

Mitchell conveyed part of Rogers's land to Stone by deed in the customary form containing covenants of title. Stone sues Rogers for breach of a covenant. The outcome of Stone's suit will be governed by whether

A. deeds without covenants are effective to convey realty.

B. the jurisdiction views the covenants as personal or running with the land.

C. Stone is a bona fide purchaser.

D. the power to "sell and convey" is construed to include the power to execute the usual form of deed used to convey realty.

91. The following are the correct ways of looking at the WTO *EXCEPT*:

    A. It's an organization for liberalizing trade.

    B. It's a forum for governments to negotiate trade agreements.

    C. It operates a system of trade rules.

    D. It is a Superman to solve all the world's problems.

92. The WTO is a place where member governments go, to try to sort out the _____ problems they face with each other.

    A. politics

    B. trade

    C. education

    D. all the above

93. Which of the following statements is *NOT* true?

    A. The WTO is just about liberalizing trade, and in some circumstances its rules support maintaining trade barriers.

    B. The WTO was born out of negotiations, and everything the WTO does is the result of negotiations.

    C. The WTO system's overriding purpose is to help trade flow as freely as possible.

    D. And it helps to settle disputes, this is a third important side to the WTO's work.

94. The regular surveillance of national trade policies through the Trade Policy Review Mechanism provides a further means of encouraging _____ both domestically and at the multilateral level.

    A. punishment

B. transparency

C. immigration

D. engagement

95. Suppose country A is better than country B at making automobiles, and country B is better than country A at making bread. It is obvious (the academics would say "trivial") that both would benefit if A specialized in automobiles, B specialized in bread and they traded their products. That is a case of _____.

   A. absolute advantage

   B. punitive damage

   C. comparative advantage

   D. comparative damage

Questions 96—100 are logical reasoning test.

96. The peculiar evil of silencing the expression of an opinion is that it robs the human race. It takes from posterity, as well as the existing generation, and from those who dissent from the opinion even more than from those who hold it. If the opinion is right, they are deprived of the opportunity of exchanging error for truth; if it is wrong, they lose what is almost as great a benefit: the clearer perception and livelier impression of truth, produced by its collision with error.

   Which one of the following best expresses the conclusion presented in the argument?

   A. Silencing the expression of an opinion is robbing the human race.

   B. Silencing the expression of an opinion harms those who dissent more than those who agree.

   C. Anyone who agrees with an opinion would not want to silence its expression.

   D. Gaining a clearer perception and livelier impression of truth is a great benefit.

97. Monroe, despite his generally poor appetite, thoroughly enjoyed the three meals he ate at the Tip-Top Restaurant, but, unfortunately, after each meal he became ill. The first time he ate an extra-large sausage pizza with a side order of hot pepper; the second time he took full advantage of the all-you-can-eat fried shrimp and hot peppers special and the third time he had two of Tip-Top's giant meatball sandwiches with hot peppers. Since the only food all three meals had in common was the hot peppers. Monroe concludes that it is solely due to Tip-Top's hot peppers that he became ill.

If both Monroe's conclusion and the evidence on which he bases it are correct, they would provide the strongest support for which one of the following?

A. Monroe can eat any of Tip-Top's daily all-you-can-eat specials without becoming ill as long as the special does not include the hot peppers.

B. If, at his third meal at Tip-Top, Monroe had chosen to eat the baked chicken with hot peppers, he would have become ill after that meal.

C. If the next time Monroe eats one of Tip-Top's extra-large sausage pizzas he does not have a side order of hot peppers, he will not become ill after his meal.

D. Before eating Tip-Top's fried shrimp with hot peppers special, Monroe had eaten fried shrimp without suffering any ill effects.

98. Investigators concluded that human failure was not responsible for the fatal airplane crash last August, and since that time new and more stringent rules for identifying and reporting mechanical problems have been in effect. That accounts for the fact that reports of airplane mechanical problems have increased in frequency by 50 percent since last August.

Which one of the following is an assumption underlying the argument in the passage?

A. Airplane travel is still relatively safe, despite the increase in reported mechanical problems.

B. Mechanical problems in airplanes have increased dramatically since last August.

C. Mechanical problems in airplanes have not increased by 50 percent since last August.

D. Airlines are less reluctant to report mechanical problems than they previously were.

99. In an effort to boost sales during the summer months, which are typically the best for soft-drink sales, Foamy Soda lowered its prices. In spite of this, however, the sales of Foamy Soda dropped during the summer months.

Each of the following, if true, contributes to reconciling the apparent discrepancy indicated above *EXCEPT*:

A. The weather during the summer months was unseasonably cool, decreasing the demand for soft drinks.

B. Foamy Soda's competitors lowered their prices even more drastically during the summer months.

C. Because of an increase in the price of sweeteners the production costs of Foamy Soda rose during the summer months.

D. A strike at Foamy Soda's main plant forced production cutbacks that resulted in many stores not receiving their normal shipments during the summer months.

100. Top college graduates are having more difficulty demonstrating their superiority to prospective employers than did the top students of twenty years ago when an honors degree was distinction enough. Today's employers are less impressed with the honors degree. Twenty years ago no more than 10 percent of a given class graduated with honors. Today, however, because of grade inflation, the honors degree goes to more than 50 percent of a graduating class. Therefore, to restore confidence in the degrees they award, colleges must take steps to control grade inflation.

Which one of the following is an assumption that, if true, would support the conclusion in the passage?

A. Awarding too many honors degrees causes colleges to inflate grades.

B. Today's students are not higher achievers than the students of twenty years ago.

C. Today's employers rely on honors ranking in making their hiring decisions.

D. Colleges must make employers aware of the criteria used to determine who receives an honors degree.

法律英语证书（LEC）全国统一考试样题
Legal English Certificate Test

PART TWO

Section I. Case Reading and Comprehension (25 points)
Read the case carefully and briefly answer the questions following the case.

Eric J. v. Betty M. (1999)
(Superior Court of Orange County, No. 718090, Gary P. Ryan, Judge.)

OPINION

When Robert was released from prison on rehabilitative parole after having been convicted of felony child molestation four years earlier, his family might have disowned him, but they didn't. They accepted him back. And when he found a girlfriend named Helen who had an eight-year-old boy named Eric they did not tell Helen about Robert's previous conviction, no doubt hoping against hope that he had reformed himself.

Unfortunately, and unbeknownst to any members of the family or Helen herself, Robert began molesting Helen's son early on in his relationship with her. Helen, acting as Eric's guardian, has now sued various members of Robert's family for not telling her of his previous conviction. Because some of the sexual abuse occurred on property owned by family members, Helen has asserted premises liability as well as general negligence as her two theories of liability.

The trial judge granted the family members' motion for nonsuit, and we now affirm the ensuing judgment. As we explain below, under the circumstances of this case, premises liability is a make-weight because there was no relationship between the harm and any premises owned by family members on which the harm occurred. The state was willing to take a chance on Robert by releasing him on parole, and so were his family members by accepting him back, so he cannot be legally equated, as Helen would have us do for purposes of premises liability, to a dangerous animal.

As to general negligence, the family members cannot be held liable for their "nonfeasance" in failing to warn Helen because to do so would contravene one of the most important, long standing, and recently reaffirmed principles of American tort law: You are not responsible for mere inaction without some sort of special relationship which creates a duty to take some action; the law does not require people to be Good Samaritans (i.e., the traditional "no duty to aid" rule).

Facts and Litigation Background

In 1978 Robert was arrested for the misdemeanor of "annoying" a minor. He pled no contest and served six months, and was on probation for the next three years. During that time he committed one probation violation for taking four high school freshman boys to dinner without supervision. Again he served some time in jail and was placed on probation.

Then in 1984 he was arrested for molesting a 10-year old boy. He again pled no contest, this time to a felony count of violating Penal Code section 288, subdivision (a) (lewd or lascivious act with or upon body of child under the age of 14). He served four years in state prison, getting out in August 1988.

In June 1989, Robert met Helen and her eight-year-old son Eric at Magic Mountain. A relationship developed between Robert and Helen, and, by Thanksgiving 1989, Robert invited Helen and Eric for an overnight stay at the home of his mother Dorothy in Big Bear so she and Eric could meet some of the rest of his family.

Besides Dorothy, Robert's family consists of his father Edwin, his father's wife Betty, Robert's three brothers Frank, Phillip and Eddie, Frank's wife Jean, and a sister named Diane. Dorothy and Diane are not parties to this appeal.

The members of Robert's family concluded that Helen was his "girlfriend."

Their relationship continued until early 1992, when Robert moved to Las Vegas.

Later that year, one of Helen's friends saw a special on television regarding convicts on parole, which showed a picture of a younger, beardless Robert and revealed that he was a convicted molester. She told Helen about the program, and a few days later, Helen took Eric to a police station. There, Helen learned that Robert had been molesting Eric. In June 1993 Robert was convicted of 23 counts of child molestation. He had never told Helen of his criminal history.

Helen, acting as guardian ad litem for Eric, sued various members of Robert's family. The case came to trial, during which it was learned that on several occasions Eric was molested on property owned by some of Robert's family members: Eric was molested at the Huntington Harbor home of Robert's father Edwin during a Christmastime gift exchange; Robert molested Eric for about two minutes while the two of them were apart from the others in a room where Frank and Jean's baby was sleeping. There were [76 Cal. App. 4th 719] several other occasions when Eric was similarly molested by Robert at Edwin and Betty's house, but the record does not reveal any more details (Eric could not recall any). Eric was also molested twice on a yacht owned by Edwin and Betty that was moored near their home. Once it was in the "driver's area" of the vessel, at a time when only Robert, Eric and a friend of Eric's named Jeff were around, and Jeff was cutting a rock with a rock cutter in front of the home, unable to see what was going on. Another time it was in the engine room of the yacht at a family gathering, when most of the members were on the dock; again the molestation lasted about two minutes.

Besides being molested at the home of Edwin and Betty several times, Eric was quickly molested once at each of the homes of Robert's three brothers: There was a birthday party at Phillip's house; the molestation took place in an entertainment room while the rest of the clan were in various other rooms. Another molestation occurred at brother Eddie's house, when Robert and Eric came to pick up some "stuff" Robert owned; at the time Eddie was working on his stereo. Similarly, when Robert and Eric came over to pick up some stuff from the home of brother Frank and his wife Jean that Robert had left, Robert molested Eric in the garage while Frank and Jean were in the house.

Each of the relatives had various degrees of knowledge of Robert's history. Father Edwin knew the most. He knew about the 1978 and 1984 convictions. Robert came to live with him and Betty for a short period after Robert's release from prison in 1988, and was visited by a parole officer shortly thereafter; she told Edwin that in her opinion Robert was a "pedophile." The parole officer also told Edwin that Robert had agreed to be put on a state parole rehabilitation program obligating him to report for psychiatric counseling, obtain gainful employment, not be alone with an unsupervised child, and allow for unannounced inspections of his residence. Edwin told Betty about the visit and the conversation.

Edwin also believed that his son was, as he would later testify in trial "truly repentant of his unfortunate situation back in 1984, that he was trying to adhere to his parole very, very vigorously." Indeed, Robert had voluntarily "participated" in the television special regarding convicts on parole against his father's advice because, as he told his father, "Dad, I want to do it to show we can succeed ..."

The parole officer also visited brother Frank and his wife Jean when she learned that Robert was going to live with them for a while. She told them [76 Cal. App. 4th 720] that Robert was a sex offender and reiterated the same parole conditions she told Edwin.

Brother Eddie learned sometime in 1989 or 1990 that Robert had been incarcerated on a molestation charge, and "wished to find out no more about it." By contrast, Robert's youngest brother Phillip thought that Robert had been in jail for kidnapping a child and understood he was on parole for that offense. He would later testify that he had "no knowledge that Bob was a felon."

The testimony was uncontroverted that none of the defendant family members ever told Helen about Robert's convictions.

After the evidence had been completed the trial court granted nonsuit motions made by the defendants in this appeal; Helen then filed a timely notice of appeal from the judgment in their favor. On appeal Helen now argues that the evidence was susceptible to liability based on either premises liability or general negligence theories.

DISCUSSION
Premises Liability

The most common situation where landowners may be held liable in tort for the criminal actions of another person on their property merely because of their status as landowners entails commercial, business or otherwise public property, with the criminal action being tied in some way to either the nature of the business or the property, and in a context where the actual perpetrator of the crimes was personally unknown to the landowner. *Frances T. v. Village Green Owners Assn. (1986) 42 Cal. 3d 490* [229 Cal. Rptr. 456, 723 P.2d 573, 59 A.L.R.4th 447] [condominium homeowners association could be held liable for rape in plaintiff's unit because of lack of exterior lighting where project had already been scene of an "exceptional crimewave"].

In "public" or business property, liability has been allowed when there is something foreseeably dangerous about the nature of the activity conducted on the property or the property itself which fixes on the landowner the duty to take some sort of precaution (e.g., Cantwell [operation of a bar]). Or the area may be such that the presence of miscreants is generally a foreseeable risk (Isaacs [drug addicts drawn to emergency room in high-crime area], Francis T. [project was experiencing "crimewave"], O'Hara [rapist targeting females in particular apartment complex], Kwaitkowski [high-crime area, previous attack], Constance B. [highways breed "highwaymen"], Zuniga [gangs in public housing project]), and Onciano [unguarded parking lot late at night fn. 6]), or the owner has in some way undertaken, as part of the organized activity on the land, care for the safety of the plaintiff as against criminal acts of third parties.

The need for a connection to the actual property itself, or some activity organized upon it, is underscored by the rationale in cases where no liability has been allowed. Absence of actual notice of any prior incidents on the property was dispositive in *Sharon P. v. Arman, Ltd. (1999) 21 Cal. 4th 1181* [91 Cal. Rptr. 2d 35, 989 P.2d 121] (absence of any assaults in previous 10 years of operation of underground parking garage), in *Ann M. v. Pacific Plaza Shopping Center, supra, 6 Cal. 4th 666* (lack of any notice by the landowner of any prior similar incidents in the subject shopping center), and in 7735 *Hollywood Blvd. Venture v. Superior Court (1981) 116 Cal. App. 3d 901* [172 Cal. Rptr. 528] (an apartment owner could not be held liable where there was no allegation that any crime had previously occurred on the premises), which appears to have adumbrated Sharon P. and Ann M. Likewise, occurrence of the crime off the premises was dispositive in *Steinmetz v. Stockton City Chamber of Commerce (1985) 169 Cal. App. 3d 1142* [214 Cal. Rptr. 405] (no liability because the assault took place in a parking lot which was not owned, possessed or controlled by the defendant), *Medina v. Hillshore Partners (1995) 40 Cal. App. 4th 477* [46 Cal. Rptr. 2d 871] (owner of an apartment complex could not be liable for an assault off the property, even though it allowed gang members to congregate on the property) and *Rosenbaum v. Security Pacific Corp. (1996) 43 Cal. App. 4th 1084* [50 Cal. Rptr. 2d 917] (owner of an apartment building could not be liable for an attack which occurred across the street from the victim's apartment [even though the victim had parked there precisely because the apartment's garage was unsafe]), again emphasizing the need for a connection to the property itself.

  As one might expect, far fewer cases involve criminal activity occurring on nonpublic residential property against social guests of the owners who live or whose tenants rent there. The typical case of premises liability in the residential context is, of course, the standard slip and fall or some other occurrence arising out of the condition of inanimate matter on the property. There do not appear to be many cases in the area involving the question of liability on the part of a landowner qua landowner for the criminal acts of unknown third persons, probably because, in the social guest-residential property context, landowners themselves actually live on the premises and are just as interested in not being assaulted as their guests.

One case relied on by Helen involving the guest-residence scenario, ***Pamela L. v. Farmer (1980) 112 Cal. App. 3d 206*** [169 Cal. Rptr. 282] (wife of sexual offender could be held liable for offenses he committed against neighborhood girls invited onto property by wife), is not really a premises liability case at all the opinion does not even mention whether the defendant there had an ownership interest in the property though the criminal acts [76 Cal. App. 4th 723] there did occur in her home and to the degree that it may be so construed, is based on the idea of the relationship of entrustment of a child which animated Wallace, the summer camp case. We address Pamela L. again in our discussion of general negligence.

The plaintiff in another guest-residence case, ***Chaney v. Superior Court (1995) 39 Cal. App. 4th 152*** [46 Cal. Rptr. 2d 73], foundered, as did the plaintiff in the commercial case of Ann M., on the defendant's actual lack of notice of the danger. In Chaney, a man molested a neighborhood girl in his home, but the defendant wife had no actual knowledge of her "husband's deviant propensities" so there was no foreseeability.

Anaya v. Turk (1984) 151 Cal. App. 3d 1092 [199 Cal. Rptr. 187] is the closest case we have found in the area because it implicates, though it does not address, the relatively complex problem which the parties have now set before us: What is the liability of a landowner qua landowner for criminal acts committed against a guest by another guest because of the criminally acting guest's prognosticated criminal "propensities"? It is a complex problem because it involves nothing less than whether landowners can incur tort liability for failing to predict the actions of a real, flesh-and-blood human being, not just a general threat of crime based on the laws of probability given statistics that the property is in a "high-crime area." And it is not a problem governed by our Supreme Court's famous decision about the future acts of a specific human being in *Tarasoff v. Regents of University of California (1976) 17 Cal. 3d 425* [131 Cal. Rptr. 14, 551 P.2d 334, 83 A.L.R.3d 1166] (psychologist could be held liable for failing to warn victim of mental patient who made threats against her), because the holding in the Tarasoff case was predicated on the fact the human being who committed the crime actually confided an intention to commit the crime prior to doing so and the psychologist to whom the confession was made was able to "in fact predict" the future occurrence of the crime. In the present case, by contrast, there is no evidence that Robert confided any intention to anybody to molest Eric; indeed, from what he told his father it is clear that he was just as intent on keeping his molestations of Eric secret from his family as from Helen.

Anaya, however, is of only limited use on the point. There, the defendants invited both the plaintiff and another guest, who was an ex-convict, to their apartment. The reason they invited the ex-convict was to sell drugs to him. The ex-convict turned violent, and shot both the plaintiff and one of the defendants. The plaintiff asserted two causes of action based on two theories [76 Cal. App. 4th 724] of liability: (a) the defendants had a duty to warn him of the other guest's "criminal propensities"; and (b) the defendants were conducting an activity (drug dealing) which increased the risk of harm to the plaintiff.

The Anaya case came to the Court of Appeal after summary judgment, and the court affirmed the judgment as to the first theory (failure to warn) which it styled as based on "mere nonfeasance (failure to intervene for the benefit of plaintiff)," reasoning that "as a matter of law" the defendants' "generalized knowledge" of the ex-convict's criminal history could not support a finding of foreseeability. "Mere knowledge that [the ex-convict] had been in federal prison did not constitute reasonable cause to anticipate his violent conduct," said the court.

The Court of Appeal reversed, however, as to the second cause of action predicated on the dangerous activity of drug dealing, because, as one expert stated in a declaration opposing the summary judgment motion, it is "a common occurrence in drug transactions that the person buying the drugs will attempt to take them by force without paying for them, and will shoot or kill anyone in his way."

While the holding of the Anaya case on the first cause of action would appear to be dispositive of any premises liability of brother Phillip, who had only the most "generalized knowledge" of Robert's past crimes, it does not speak to the other defendants here, who all knew at least (in contrast with the defendants in Anaya) what Robert had been convicted of. Nor is its holding on the second cause of action much use: Family gatherings are most assuredly not drug deals, and there is nothing in this case to suggest that absent the mere fact the Robert and Eric (and often Helen) would show up together there was any activity conducted by any of the defendants on the premises that would increase the risk. Robert's family could hardly be responsible for supervising him every moment during an innocent family gathering such as a Christmas gift exchange.

What Anaya does is to make reference to the plaintiff's "contention" that the ex-convict's "dangerous propensities" established some sort of duty on the part of the landowner, though the opinion never explores the idea of the "dangerous propensities" of specific human beings in detail.

There was obviously a subtext, however, that ran through the plaintiff's argument in Anaya, that Stanley Wilsonthe ex-convict in the case was [76 Cal. App. 4th 725] the functional equivalent of a dangerous animal. The argument is even closer to the surface in the present case, where the leitmotif of Helen's appellate argument is that Robert because he had once been convicted of felony child molestation and once been convicted of misdemeanor annoyance of a child was, when he was on the defendants' property, to be treated as if he were a vicious pit bull, for whom a landowner might be liable just for allowing it on the landowner's property.

Now, maybe in retrospect Robert was the moral equivalent of a vicious pit bull, and there is no doubt that, as a sex offender, he represented a threat. But to say that his convictions made him for purposes of the tort liability of his fellow family members who didn't turn him away after his crime the equivalent of a brute beast without the capacity to repent, does not square with the parole scheme under which Robert was released.

The academic criminologist, James Q. Wilson, once observed that belief in rehabilitation "requires not merely optimistic but heroic assumptions about the nature of man." It may have been woolly thinking to release Robert in 1988, but he was released, and released under the auspices of a state parole rehabilitation program. Perhaps when he was convicted of felony child molestation in 1984 he should have been incarcerated for life without possibility of parole (i.e., locked up and the key thrown away), but that was not what the law of criminal sentencing provided. When Robert was released rehabilitation was the goal, and it cannot be said as a matter of law, even in the case of individuals who have been convicted of felony child molestation, that the rate of recidivism in such cases is 100 percent. The legislative goal of rehabilitation embodied in the very fact that Robert was indeed released on parole cannot be squared, for purposes of landowner liability, with the assumption that Robert was the legal equivalent of a dangerous animal.

The problem of predicting when a specific convict will again commit a crime was confronted by our Supreme Court in ***Thompson v. County of Alameda (1980) 27 Cal. 3d 741*** (albeit not in the context of premises liability), which involved stronger facts than those before us. There, a county released a juvenile offender with "latent, extremely dangerous and violent propensities regarding young children" (as he was described in the complaint) on temporary leave to his mother's custody even though the county knew that he would, if released, "take the life of a young child residing in the neighborhood." (Id. at p. 746.) After the offender did just that, and murdered a child of neighbors just a few doors down, the parents of the victim sued the county for failing to warn them of the offender's "propensities." (Ibid.)

The Supreme Court affirmed a judgment after a demurrer was sustained without leave to amend, and specifically tackled the "troublesome" problem of whether the county had a duty to warn. Justice Richardson, writing for the court majority, first noted that "a large number of parole violations occur." Releasing the offender was fraught with the possibility of recidivism. But the fact that the Legislature had provided for parole and probation release programs showed that it was willing to accept the risk the "rehabilitative effort will fail" to gain the benefit that at least some parolees would be returned to a "productive position in society." (Ibid.) Because the case involved only "nonspecific threats of harm directed at nonspecific victims" the court concluded that as a matter of law there was no duty on the part of the county to warn of the release of "an inmate with a violent history." Essentially, noted the court, the Legislature had made a value judgment, and that judgment had certain consequences: "Obviously aware of the risk of failure of probation and parole programs the Legislature has nonetheless as a matter of public policy elected to continue those programs even though such risks must be borne by the public."

If the Legislature was prepared to accept the possibility of Robert's rehabilitation, he cannot be equated with an inanimate, dangerous condition, or that of a dangerous animal. This is not a case of keeping a dog which is likely to attack someone on a piece of property.

Given that Robert's mere presence on the property cannot be considered a dangerous condition of the property, there is no basis for premises liability. Nor do any of the other bases for premises liability apply. There was nothing about the nature of any activity conducted on the property to implicate such liability again, family gatherings cannot be equated with drug dealing or operating a bar open to the public. Nor was there anything about the nature of any of the properties owned by the defendants to implicate liability they were just homes, and in the case of Robert's father, a yacht. Nor was there any relationship of entrustment of a child by virtue of an activity conducted on the premises, such as happened in Wallace, the summer camp case. If anyone was responsible for Eric, even at the family gatherings or times when Robert came over to his brothers to pick up his "stuff," it was Helen. We therefore conclude that the trial court correctly granted the nonsuit motion as to Helen's premises liability theory.

General Negligence

Absent a "special relationship," one cannot be held liable for mere nonfeasance, such as not protecting another from a criminal attack by a third party. The basic idea is often referred to as the "no duty to aid rule," which remains a fundamental and long-standing rule of tort law. As the Supreme Court said in ***Williams v. State of California (1983) 34 Cal. 3d 18, 23*** [192 Cal. Rptr. 233, 664 P.2d 137]: "As a rule, one has no duty to come to the aid of another. A person who has not created a peril is not liable in tort merely for failure to take affirmative action to assist or protect another unless there is some relationship between them which gives rise to a duty to act."

To the degree that Helen asserts a cause of action for negligence disconnected from premises liability, her claim essentially requires this court to depart from the rule against liability for mere nonfeasance. That rule is foundational in California tort jurisprudence. The tort law of California does not impose mandatory Good Samaritanism. In light of the reaffirmation of that rule as late as recently as 1983 in Williams (and impliedly in 1994 in Heitzman as well), we decline to do so.

Helen argues that ***Soldano v. O'Daniels (1983) 141 Cal. App. 3d 443***, modified the no duty to aid rule. As one commentator has noted, Soldano stands out as the only case in the United States during the 30-year period since the death of Kitty Genovese that could "be read" as adopting a duty to aid rule, though the commentator who made that statement also noted that the "court's apparent holding [was] to the contrary."

Soldano did not abrogate the rule against liability for mere nonfeasance. Rather like Justice Scalia's observation about the famous contracts case of ***Hadley v. Baxendale (1854) 156 Eng. Rep. 145***, it is an instance of a court knowing the right rule but simply not applying it correctly. The time has come to explain why the result in case is an aberration in American tort jurisprudence.

In Soldano, a saloon patron ran across the street to a restaurant to try to phone the police about a threat that had been made in the bar. The patron requested the bartender of the restaurant (in the fairly neutral language which the opinion used to describe the actual facts) to "either call the police or allow him to use the [restaurant] phone to call the police. That [bartender] allegedly refused to call the police and allegedly refused to allow the patron to use the phone to make his own call." The threat in the saloon eventually escalated into a lethal shooting.

The appellate court reversed the judgment entered after a summary judgment motion when the son of the man who was shot and killed in the saloon sued the restaurant across the street. The appellate court began its substantive discussion by saying the "facts" of the case before it "come very nearly within section 327" of the Restatement Second of Torts, which the court then [76 Cal. App. 4th 729] paraphrased for the rather noncontroversial point that if you know a third person is going to render aid to another you shouldn't "prevent" that person "from doing so." The opinion then quoted from a scope note making the same point, except it added the idea that you shouldn't "interfere" with another person's attempt to give aid as well as "prevent" it.

The problem with the court's analysis is that it subtly equated the concepts of prevention and interference as used in section 327 of the Restatement Second of Torts with the fact that the bartender had refused to allow a saloon patron from across the street use the restaurant's phone. Interference and refusal to allow one's property to be commandeered, even for a good purpose, are simply two different things. If the English words "prevent" and "interfere" still mean anything, they necessarily convey the notion of some sort of affirmative action, not just refusal to turn one's property over to someone else.

In addition to Soldano, Helen also relies on *Pamela L. v. Farmer, supra, 112 Cal. App. 3d 206*, which, as we noted above, is another general negligence case, not a premises liability one. In Pamela L., the appellate court held that the wife of a "sexual offender [who] had molested women and children in the past" could be held liable for telling the parents of three children that it would be "safe for them to play at her house." The court distinguished the case from the traditional "nonfeasance cases" because the wife's affirmative representations increased the likelihood of harm. Indeed, she specifically invited the children to her home and thereby "assumed" a "special relationship." In essence, Pamela L. is a negligent or intentional misrepresentation case, not a failure to warn case at all. It is obvious that the wife in Pamela L. was seen by the court as functioning as a procurer of victims for her husband. Here, by contrast, Helen has pointed to no affirmative misrepresentations as to how "safe" Eric might have been if left alone with Robert; nor does she make any suggestion that family members were acting to facilitate any molestation.

Helen invites us to consider the duty question here under the traditional seven factors used by the courts. That weighing process, however, has already been done by courts over the centuries in [76 Cal. App. 4th 730] formulating the "no duty to aid" rule. We need only add that any result other than the one we reach today under the facts of this case would create intolerable conflicts of interest within families.

CONCLUSION

The judgment in favor of the respondents is affirmed. Because we affirm the judgment, the protective cross-appeal is moot.

Rylaarsdam, J., and Bedsworth, J., concurred.

Question: Please write a case brief.

Section II. Legal Translation (40 points)
A. Please translate the following Chinese into English.

居间合同

第四百二十四条　居间合同是居间人向委托人报告订立合同的机会

或者提供订立合同的媒介服务，委托人支付报酬的合同。

第四百二十五条　居间人应当就有关订立合同的事项向委托人如实报告。

居间人故意隐瞒与订立合同有关的重要事实或者提供虚假情况，损害委托人利益的，不得要求支付报酬并应当承担损害赔偿责任。

第四百二十六条　居间人促成合同成立的，委托人应当按照约定支付报酬。对居间人的报酬没有约定或者约定不明确，依照本法第六十一条的规定仍不能确定的，根据居间人的劳务合理确定。因居间人提供订立合同的媒介服务而促成合同成立的，由该合同的当事人平均负担居间人的报酬。

居间人促成合同成立的，居间活动的费用，由居间人负担。

第四百二十七条　居间人未促成合同成立的，不得要求支付报酬，但可以要求委托人支付从事居间活动支出的必要费用。

B. Please translate the following paragraphs into Chinese.

The United States District Court for the District for Columbia has largely decided the first litigated case testing the President's authority to block or unwind foreign acquisitions of U.S. businesses. The court's decision, in Ralls Corporation v. Committee on Foreign Investment in the United States, reaffirmed the President's broad authority to restrict foreign investment in U.S. businesses through the CFIUS process without judicial review. The decision also holds that the President may structure divestiture orders to require ancillary remedial actions (as long as they are reasonably related to implementation of the divestiture order itself). The court left open the question whether CFIUS itself can issue unilateral "interim" orders that exercise these presidential powers pending the President's decision whether to act. It also reserved the question whether the President could be required to explain the reasoning for his blockage/divestiture decisions sufficiently to allow the prospective foreign investor to respond to (and perhaps to overcome) his concerns. While the Ralls decision remains subject to appellate review, it is unlikely to discourage CFIUS's more aggressive recent approach to foreign investment transactions that CFIUS concludes pose a risk to U.S. national security.

CFIUS is the interagency Executive Branch committee that considers the impact on US national security of "any merger, acquisition, or takeover... by or with a foreign person which could result in foreign control of any person engaged in interstate commerce in the United States." Through its review, CFIUS determines whether the transaction poses a threat to national security interests, and whether to recommend that the President therefore block the transaction on those grounds. The President then is authorized (but not required) to "take such action for such time as the President considers appropriate to suspend or prohibit any covered transaction that threatens to impair the national security of the United States."

Ralls involved a Chinese investor's indirect purchase of four wind energy farms in the state of Oregon. The purchase closed without CFIUS review, in light of the apparently benign character of the business segment in which the target operated, but it turned out that one of the wind farm project sites was located near air space used by the U.S. Navy for flight testing and other sensitive military training. When the Government learned of the transaction after it closed, discussions within the Government led to a CFIUS request to the parties for a filing. That filing led to CFIUS review and, ultimately, issuance of an interim order by CFIUS, and then a final order by the President, that respectively imposed restrictions on the investor's control of the target pending presidential decision, and later divestiture order (coupled with ancillary implementing restrictions).

Section III. Legal Writing (35 Points)

Suppose you are Ben Warrington, a law clerk with the White & Himmelman law firm in Seattle, Washington. Philip and Julia Lang own a nursery that sells plants, trees, and gardening equipment. Last spring, they received a shipment of young spruce trees and had no space for all of them in the nursery. They planted ten of the trees in the backyard of their residence, four feet apart, with the intention of moving them to the nursery as soon as there was space available. Two months later they sold their residence to Wilbur and Marcie Richards, who did not plan to move into the residence until the fall. During the negotiations, no mention was made of the spruce trees. The Langs did not remove the trees prior to the sale because there was still no room in the nursery, but they planned to do so before the Richards moved in. The Richards assumed that the trees were part of the realty that they bought and have refused to allow the Langs to remove them. The Langs have consulted you regarding the ownership of the trees. You have found two cases in your jurisdiction.

Stafford National Bank v. Dinesen (1958)

Eric Dinesen owned property, including 30 acres of bogs, on which he grew cranberry bushes. He defaulted on a mortgage held by Stafford National Bank, and the bank now has title to the real estate. Dinesen attempted to dig up and transplant the cranberry bushes to another tract of land he owns and the bank filed suit, claiming that the bushes are part of the real estate and no longer Dinesen's property. Dinesen appeals from the trial court's decision awarding ownership of the cranberry bushes to the bank.

This is a case of first impression in this state. At common law, whatever was affixed to the land, including plants and trees, was part of the land. Crops, however, even though growing in the soil, were considered personalty if that was the intent of the owner. The cranberry bushes in this case are not crops because there is no intent to harvest them annually. The purpose is to harvest the berries, not the plants themselves. The bushes are therefore part of the realty and belong to the bank. Affirmed.

Updike v. Teague (1955)

Leslie Updike's action against William Teague for the conversion of nursery stock was dismissed by the trial court for failure to state a cause of action. Updike had entered into a contract with Teague for the sale of certain real estate. After Updike defaulted on the contract, Teague took possession of the land.

Updike owned a nursery, which was located on the property. He supplied orchards with fruit trees and used the land to grow young trees for resale. After the default, Teague refused to allow Updike to remove the nursery stock and sold it himself. Updike claims the trees are his personal property because he did not intend for them to be part of the realty. He stated that the trees were planted close together in rows and that the planting was temporary, usually for no longer than a year, and for the purpose of maintaining them until they were sold.

The trial court applied the traditional common law rule that plants and trees growing in the soil are part of the land and belong to the landowner. We believe these trees are more property characterized as stock in trade, which is defined as goods and chattels that a merchant obtains for the purpose of resale and is considered personal property. Trees offered for sale must necessarily be kept in the soil. Updike placed them there for the sole purpose of keeping them alive prior to sale. They were therefore the personal property of Updike. Reversed.

Please use these facts and the case authorities above to draft a 600- to 800-word office memo to Frank Zhang, a senior partner in your firm.

1. Describe the issue here in this problem.
2. Describe the court's holding in the case, *Stafford National Bank v. Dinesen (1958)*.
3. Describe the court's holding in the case, *Updike v. Teague (1955)*.
4. Describe the rule of law applicable to the issue in this problem.
5. Describe what would be the result of the court's decision in this problem based on law found in the *Stafford National Bank v. Dinesen* and *Updike v. Teague* cases.

法律英语证书（LEC）全国统一考试样题
参考答案

PART ONE

1	A	21	A	41	D	61	D	81	B
2	C	22	A	42	C	62	A	82	B
3	C	23	C	43	D	63	C	83	A
4	B	24	A	44	D	64	B	84	C
5	A	25	C	45	A	65	A	85	B
6	A	26	C	46	B	66	A	86	B
7	A	27	B	47	D	67	B	87	B
8	B	28	A	48	D	68	C	88	C
9	C	29	D	49	A	69	B	89	B
10	C	30	B	50	A	70	D	90	D
11	D	31	A	51	A	71	C	91	A
12	B	32	D	52	C	72	B	92	B
13	C	33	D	53	C	73	A	93	A
14	D	34	B	54	D	74	A	94	B
15	A	35	C	55	D	75	A	95	A
16	D	36	A	56	B	76	D	96	A
17	A	37	A	57	A	77	D	97	B
18	C	38	C	58	A	78	A	98	C
19	B	39	D	59	B	79	B	99	C
20	C	40	A	60	D	80	D	100	B

PART TWO

Section I. Case Reading and Comprehension
FACTS

Robert brought home his new girlfriend, Helen, and her eight-year-old son, Eric, to meet his mother, father, brothers, and sister and their spouses. The relationship between Robert and Helen continued and Helen and Eric were guests several times in different family homes. No family member told Helen about Robert's criminal history of felony child molestation. It was later discovered that Robert sexually molested Eric during some of these visits at the family homes all the while Robert was on parole for child molestation. Robert was convicted of molesting Eric and sent back to prison. Helen filed suit against Robert's family claiming they had a duty to warn her about Robert's criminal past and the potential danger to her child, and failing that duty they were liable for money damages for the harm suffered by Eric. The trial court dismissed the case on a nonsuit motion.

ISSUE

Whether the trial court properly dismissed the negligence claim based on the premise that family members of a convicted child molester have no affirmative duty to disclose that information to the molester's girlfriend who has an eight-year-old boy.

HOLDING

The appellate court affirmed the trial court, holding that the family members had no affirmative duty to disclose the information.

RATIONALE

The appellate court placed great weight upon the "no duty to aid" rule, developed "over the centuries" in courts. The court noted that a special relationship is required to create a duty to warn, give aid, or otherwise help another. Ultimately, the court found that no such special relationship existed and found no other reason to suggest that the family members had a duty to warn the girlfriend. The court cited several cases, including a California Supreme Court case, Williams v. State of California, that establish the "no duty to aid" rule. In short, a person who has not created the danger or risk is not liable simply for failing to take an affirmative action unless there is "some relationship" that creates a "duty to act." The court rejected a case that seemed to rule the other way, Soldano v. O'Daniels, by explaining that the facts in that case clearly showed that the defendant had actually prevented someone else from rendering aid. The court also noted that any decision to find a duty to aid in this case would interfere with family relationships by creating "intolerable conflicts of interest." Impliedly, this went against public policy.

Section II. Legal Translation
A. Please translate the following Chinese into English.

Contracts for Intermediation

Article 424 An intermediation contract refer to a contract where-by the intermediator reports to the principal the opportunity for concluding a contract or provides intermediate service for concluding a contract, and the principal pays the remuneration.

Article 425 The intermediator shall report truthfully to the principal the matters related to the conclusion of a contract.

Where the intermediator intentionally conceals the important facts relating to the conclusion of the contract or provides false information and harms the interests of the principal, the said party may not claim the payment of remuneration and shall be liable for damages.

Article 426 The principal shall pay the intermediator remuneration according to the terms of the contract if the intermediator has facilitated the establishment of a contract. Where there is no such agreement in the contract on remuneration or such agreement is unclear, nor can it be determined according to the provisions of Article 61 of this Law, the remuneration shall be determined reasonably according to the service rendered by the intermediator. If the establishment of a contract has been facilitated by the intermediate service rendered by the intermediator, the remuneration shall be borne equally by the parties to the contract.

Where the intermediator has facilitated the conclusion of the contract, the expenses for the intermediate service shall be borne by the intermediator.

Article 427 Where the intermediator fails in facilitating the conclusion of a contract, the intermediator may not request for the payment of remuneration, but may request the principal to pay the necessary expenses for the intermediate service.

B. Please translate the following paragraphs into Chinese.

对总统是否拥有阻止或否决外资收购美国企业的权力，美国哥伦比亚地区法院已经很大程度上在第一起类似诉讼案中做出了基本判决。奥斯公司诉美国外国投资委员会一案的法院判决则重新确定了总统可以通过外国投资委员会审查程序而不经过司法审查直接限制外资向美国企业投资的广泛权力。该判决还认可总统可以发出撤销命令，要求采取附加救济措施（只要这些救济措施与执行撤销命令有关）。法院悬而未决的一个问题是：在总统还未决定是否做出上述决定之前，美国外国投资委员会是否可以行使该总统权力单方发布"临时"禁令。同时，另一个问题是：能否要求总统对其做出阻止投资或者撤销命令的依据进行详尽的解释，以便未来外国投资者能面对（或者解决）总统的这些担忧。尽管奥斯一案的判决仍然处于上诉阶段，但这已不太可能阻止美国外国投资委员会最近对其认为可能威胁美国国家安全的外资交易采取的日趋激进的做法。

美国外国投资委员会是一个具有跨部门行政性质的委员会，负责衡量"外国人进行的或与外国人进行的、可能导致美国州际业务受制于外资的任何合并、收购或并购"对美国国家安全的影响。通过审查，美国外国投资委员会可以确定某个交易是否对美国国家安全构成威胁，是否建议总统因此阻止该项交易。总统由此被授权（但不被要求）"采取总统认为合适的措施中止或禁止任何有可能损害美国国家安全的相关交易"。

罗尔斯一案涉及一名中国投资人间接购买位于俄勒冈州的四家风电场。因为目标公司显著的商业优势,上述交易在未经美国外国投资委员会审查的情况下完成了。但结果是,其中一处风电场项目位于美国海军用于飞行测试和其他敏感军事训练的空军基地附近。交易结束后美国政府得悉这一消息,并在内部展开了讨论,结果是美国外国投资委员会要求交易双方进行申报。申报后,美国外国投资委员会进行了审查,并发布了临时禁令,而总统则签署了最终禁令。两则命令都限制投资人在总统签署禁令及后来的撤销收购令(包括实施相应的限制)前控制目标公司。

Section III. Legal Writing

写作提示:法律文书的写作力求思路清晰、表达准确并且通俗易懂。无论是律师信函、法律备忘录,还是案件辩论书都有严格的写作格式需要遵循,这对考生来说是至关重要的一点。在篇幅上,要按题目要求的字数完成写作。另外,还要注意英文书写工整,尽量避免语法、拼写错误。

按照题目要求写一篇600—800字的法律备忘录,注意备忘录的写作格式,文中要包含如下内容:

1. Describe the issue here in this problem.

    The issue is whether the spruce trees are personal property of the Langs and can be removed by them.

2. Describe the court's holding in the case, **Stafford National Bank v. Dinesen (1958)**.

    The court held that the bushes are part of the realty and belonged to the bank.

3. Describe the court's holding in the case, **Updike v. Teague (1955)**.

    The court held that the trees growing in the soil are for the sole purpose of keeping them alive prior to the sale, and thus are considered as personal property.

4. Describe the rule of law applicable to the issue in this problem.

Under common law, the general rule is that trees growing in the soil are part of the land or realty. However, there is an exception where the crops are considered personal property if the owner so intended. An additional exception to this rule is that trees or plants that are stock in trade are the merchant's personal property; stock in trade is defined as "goods or chattel that a merchant obtains for the purpose of resale."

5. Describe what would be the result of the court's decision in this problem based on law found in the **Stafford National Bank v. Dinesen** and **Updike v. Teague** cases.

The likely result is that the court will find that the spruce trees are the Langs' personal property as these were intended to be the stock and trade of their business, and are supposed to be offered for the purpose of resale, and therefore are not considered as part of the real estate sold to the Richards.

* HOW TO BRIEF

Case briefs are a necessary study aid in law school that helps to encapsulate and analyze the mountainous mass of material that law students must digest. The case brief represents a final product after reading a case, rereading it, taking it apart, and putting it back together again. In addition to its function as a tool for self-instruction and referencing, the case brief also provides a valuable "cheat sheet" for class participation.

What are the elements of a brief? Different people will tell you to include different things in your brief. Most likely, upon entering law school, this will happen with one or more of your instructors. While opinions may vary, four elements that are essential to any useful brief are the following:

(a) Facts (name of the case and its parties, what happened factually and procedurally, and the judgment)
(b) Issues (what is in dispute)
(c) Holding (the applied rule of law)
(d) Rationale (reasons for the holding)

In addition to these elements, it may help you to organize your thoughts, as some people do, by dividing Facts into separate elements:
(1) Facts of the case (what actually happened, the controversy)
(2) Procedural History (what events within the court system led to the present case)
(3) Judgment (what the court actually decided)

Procedural History is usually minimal and most of the time irrelevant to the ultimate importance of a case; however, this is not always true. One subject in which Procedure History is virtually always relevant is Civil Procedure.

When describing the Judgment of the case, distinguish it from the Holding. The Judgment is the factual determination by the court, in favor of one party, such as "affirmed" "reversed" or "remanded." In contrast, the Holding is the applied rule of law that serves as the basis for the ultimate judgment.

Your brief shouldn't exceed 600 words, excluding concurrences and dissents.

2018年11月法律英语证书（LEC）全国统一考试试题及参考答案

试 卷 一

提示：本试卷为选择题，由计算机阅改。请将所选答案填涂在答题卡上，勿在卷面上直接作答。

本卷为单项选择题，每题所给的选项中只有一个正确或最好答案。每题1分，共100分。

1. Incapacity

    A. The inability to deliver merchandise promised in a contract.

    B. A voluntary transfer, by a debtor of all his property to a trustee for the benefit of all his creditors.

    C. A defense to contract liability, such as being too young.

    D. Someone who gives assistance to the perpetrator of crime, without directly committing it, sometimes without being present.

2. Detrimental Reliance

    A. Political or social union of contracting parties.

    B. A statement that denies something, especially responsibility.

    C. The process of gathering and preserving evidence prior to trial in a civil or criminal case.

---

① 2018年11月法律英语证书（LEC）全国统一考试尚未采用机考，故题目型式与样题略有出入。

D. Reliance that may result in promissory estoppel.

3. Paralegal

   A. A lawyer's assistant.

   B. One who holds an advanced law degree.

   C. A person who persuades or influences someone to do something, especially enter into a contract.

   D. Formally, by a grand jury, accuse or charge someone with a crime.

4. Conversion

   A. Procedure that allows offenders to return to prison.

   B. The wrongful exercise of the right of ownership or control over goods which belong to another.

   C. Constitutional Amendment that made it a crime to drink alcohol.

   D. Denoting an action or the bringer of an action that is brought without sufficient grounds for winning, purely to cause annoyance to the defendant.

5. Contraband

   A. A musical group from Nicaragua, popular during the 1980's.

   B. Any property, such as narcotics or weapons, which is unlawful to produce, possess, or smuggle.

   C. The authority of a court to review the official actions of other branches of government.

   D. The constitutional power of the U.S. President to banish criminals who displease him.

6. Attorney General

   A. A military attorney who represents the U.S. Armed Forces.

   B. An attorney who does not have a specialty in law but rather maintains a general law practice.

   C. A person appointed by the court to appear on behalf of a minor or incompetent person who is a plaintiff in a civil action.

D. On the federal level, the attorney who is the head of the U.S. Department of Justice, and on the state level, the attorney who represents the state in court proceedings and other legal matters.

7. Directed Verdict

    A. A wrongful verdict by a jury.

    B. A ruling by a judge that the evidence so overwhelmingly favors one party that it is not even necessary for the jury to make a decision.

    C. Basic principles of law generally accepted by the courts or embodied in the statutes of a particular jurisdiction.

    D. In criminal cases, reasonable grounds for believing that the facts justify issuance of an arrest or search warrant, or further legal action.

8. De Facto

    A. Latin words means to start over from beginning.

    B. Latin expression means "actual" (if used as an adjective) or "in practice" (if used as an adverb).

    C. A declaration of a statement's truth, which renders one willfully asserting an untrue statement punishable for perjury.

    D. The rule preventing illegally obtained evidence, such as property found during an illegal search, from being used in any trial.

9. Ab Initio

    A. A legal term means "from the beginning."

    B. A legal term from the Latin meaning literally, "the thing itself speaks" but is more often translated "the thing speaks for itself."

    C. The prosecutor declines to prosecute, but may still initiate prosecution within the time allowed by law.

    D. A term used to describe permanent and absolute tenure of land or property with freedom to dispose of it at will.

10. Proximate Cause

    A. An actual cause that is also legally sufficient to support liability.

B. A motion by a defense attorney in a civil action.

C. A good reason to sue a person for committing an intentional tort.

D. Basic principles of law generally accepted by the courts or embodied in the statutes of a particular jurisdiction.

11. Which of the following statements is *NOT* true in the United States?

    A. The U.S. legal system is a complex organization of federal and state governmental divisions.

    B. The U.S. Constitution is the highest law of the land, federal laws enacted by the U.S. Congress come next. This means that the Federal Congress can adopt laws that control states in every situation.

    C. Federal and state courts exist side by side. State courts are courts of general jurisdiction and decide many more cases than federal court. The federal courts' jurisdiction is much more limited than the state courts' jurisdiction.

    D. Each state has a legislature that adopts state laws called "statutes." Those statutes are sometimes complied into what is referred to as a code. This is nothing more than a codification of all the applicable statutes.

12. People who commit _____ may be issued a summons, while anyone committing a _____ is arrested.

    A. misdemeanors, felony

    B. crimes, misdemeanor

    C. murder, manslaughter

    D. theft, minor offence

13. An appellate court's decision on an issue is binding on lower courts in the appellate court's jurisdiction. Thus, an appellate court's decisions are _____ that the lower courts in the appellate court's jurisdiction must follow.

    A. black letter law

B. precedent

C. stare Decisis

D. model code

14. Which of the following statements is *NOT* true in the United States?

    A. Because the United States Supreme Court is the highest court in the land, the Supreme Court's decisions are binding on all courts in the United States.

    B. Two requirements are the most important in law school admission: the applicant's undergraduate GPA and scores on the LSAT.

    C. Law Reviews are legal academic journals edited and in part written by JD students.

    D. In the United States, many arbitration cases are handled by arbitrators approved by the American Bar Association, which has offices in a number of cites.

15. The U. S. Constitution provides a list of congressional powers as the following *EXCEPT* _____ .

    A. collection of taxes

    B. repayment of common defense

    C. establishment of inferior courts

    D. issuance of green cards

16. The executive branch of the United States Government consists of _____ .

    A. the president

    B. vice President

    C. fifteen cabinet-level executive departments

    D. all of the above

Questions 17—19 are based on the following fact situation:

Congress enacted legislation that was intended to open up federal lands to private industry to explore for, and extract, oil and coal deposits. The act established the Federal Lands Exploitation Commission to supervise the exploration and extraction of fossil fuels from federal lands, and empowered the Commission to enter into contracts on behalf of the federal government with private companies that wish to mine for coal and drill for oil. The Commission members were also required to investigate safe and sound methods of exploiting the oil and coal deposits without doing unnecessary harm to the environment and to make recommendations to Congress for new laws that would govern the exploitation of federal lands. Further, the commissioners were given the power to make the rules and regulations concerning the contracts with the companies and to appoint administrative law judges to conduct hearings regarding violation of the Commission's rules and disputes concerning the contracts.

The Commission's chairperson was designated as an Undersecretary of the Interior; the President appointed two commissioners from environmental groups; and the oil and coal companies selected one commissioner each, who were then appointed by Congress to the Commission.

17. The authority for the establishment of the Federal Lands Exploitation Commission is most likely

   A. the Commerce Clause.

   B. the taxing and spending power.

   C. Congress's authority to regulate federal land.

   D. the war and defense power.

18. For its violation of the Commission's rules with regard to pollution of water resulting from drilling operations, AmOil was fined $5,000. AmOil files suit in the federal court to enjoin the Commission's enforcement of this rule. AmOil's best argument in support of its contention that the rule was illegal is that

   A. regulations concerning criminal conduct cannot be made by agency rules, but must be made by federal statute.

   B. the appointment of the commissioners was illegal; therefore, the rules promulgated by the Commission are invalid.

C. since the fine was potentially $5,000 for violation of the rule, AmOil had a right to a trial by jury, which was denied when the matter was heard by the administrative law judge.

D. the proceeding before the administrative law judge violated AmOil's rights of equal protection as guaranteed by the Fourteenth Amendment.

19. Administrative Law Judge May had been appointed to his position by a former Undersecretary of the Interior who was the Commission chairperson. When the new administration came into office, the new Commission chairperson removed May from his position as the ALJ, but offered May a position as an attorney in the enforcement division. May brought suit in the federal court to enjoin the Commission chairperson from removing him from his position. May should

A. prevail, because a judge cannot be removed from office after appointment.

B. prevail, if it is shown that all times he maintained good behavior.

C. not prevail, because he was not a judge within the meaning of Article III.

D. not prevail, because the appointing authority had changed.

Questions 20—21 are based on the following fact situation:

The President of the United States and the Prime Minister of Canada, recognizing a growing problem involving the killing of baby harp seals, agreed that each should appoint three members to a special commission to look into the problem. The commission was instructed to make a comprehensive study of the baby harp seal problem and to draft regulations that would provide for the preservation of the seal population while still allowing fur traders to take a certain number of furs each year. After studying the problem, the commission drafted proposed regulations and submitted them to the President and the Prime Minister. The President of the United States, acting in concert with the Prime Minster of Canada, named the commission as a permanent enforcement agency for the regulations that were adopted by both nations.

附录一
2018 年 11 月法律英语证书（LEC）全国统一考试试题及参考答案

The President, acting with prior congressional authorization, then entered into an executive agreement with the Prime Minister whereby the joint commission was granted adjudicative as well as enforcement powers with respect to the regulation of baby harp seals.

20. The executive agreement by the President is

   A. valid, because the President has unlimited powers in entering into executive agreements.

   B. valid, because the President has plenary powers in the area of foreign affairs.

   C. invalid, unless the Senate ratified the executive agreement by a two-thirds vote.

   D. invalid, because conservation of wildlife is not an area left solely to Presidential discretion.

21. Assume that the joint commission adopted a regulation whereby all baby harp seal hunters were restricted to taking furs between December 1 and April 30 of each year, and that each hunter could take no more than one baby harp seal fur per day. Assume further that the state of Maine adopted a statute requiring baby harp seal hunters to register the state and obtain a special hunting license that allowed the year-round hunting of baby harp seals, for the price of $5,000. The joint commission filed an action in federal district court seeking to enjoin Maine from enforcing the statute. The district court most likely would declare the state statute to be

   A. constitutional, because the conversation of wildlife is an issue best left to the states in which the wildlife are located.

   B. constitutional, because a state statute takes precedence over any executive agreement.

   C. unconstitutional, because an executive agreement is the law of the land, and any acts by a state inconsistent therewith are null and void.

   D. unconstitutional, because the state statute discriminates against baby harp seal hunters from the state of Maine.

22. In an effort to protect the dwindling California condor population, Congress enacted the Condor Preservation Act, which made it illegal to take, possess, or sell any part of a California condor. The constitutionality of the Act is challenged by Zephyr, a seller of gifts and artifacts, including artifacts made out of California condor feathers.

    Is the Act valid?

    A. No, the statute violates due process because the absolute prohibition on sale is an effective taking under the Fifth Amendment Due Process Clause without just compensation.

    B. No, because the statute is discriminatory as applied.

    C. Yes, because the regulation is rationally related to interstate commerce.

    D. Yes, because the statute is designed to protect a dwindling national resource.

23. Broad Acres is a housing development of one-, two-, and three-bedroom units. All units are suitable for occupancy, and the developers of the project have filed the appropriate documents and deeds, including a Declaration of Restrictions that limits ownership and occupancy of the units to families or to groups of unrelated adults of not more than three in number. Each deed to the individual units contains the following statement:

    As shown on recorded plat (page and plat book reference) and subject to the restrictions stated therein.

    One of the two-bedroom units was purchased by Dora and her boyfriend Greg. They immediately moved into the unit with another unmarried couple who were friends of theirs. Other unit owners brought suit against Dora and Greg to enjoin the occupancy by the other couple.

    If judgment is in favor of Dora and Greg, the issue that most likely would determine this result is whether

    A. the restriction constitutes an unlawful restraint against alienation.

    B. enforcement of the restriction would violate the Equal Protection

Clause of the Fourteenth Amendment.

C. notice was given by Dora and Greg to the sellers of the unit that they intended to occupy the residence with another couple.

D. a two-bedroom unit can comfortably contain a group of four adults.

24. Foley was a permanent resident alien of the United States who was awaiting an opportunity to become a citizen. Foley filed an application to become an instructor in the local public high school but was denied the position solely on the ground that he was not a citizen. Foley now brings suit, alleging that his status as a resident alien was not a proper ground for denying him a position as an instructor.

    May the state deny a permanent resident alien employment as an instructor in the public high school?

    A. Yes, because employment by the state is a privilege, not a right.

    B. Yes, because citizenship bears some rational relationship to the interest that is being protected.

    C. No, to do so would be a denial of equal protection.

    D. No, because the evidence presented was uncontroverted that he was awaiting the opportunity to become a citizen.

25. City passed a municipal ordinance that prohibited door-to-door solicitation of contributions by charitable organizations that did not use at least 75% of their receipts for "charitable purpose." The ordinance further provided that anyone wishing to solicit for purposes of charity must obtain a permit and present satisfactory proof that at least 75% of the proceeds of such solicitation shall be used directly for the charitable purposes of the organization. The Citizens for an Easier Passing, a corporation organized to promote "the knowledge and the use of accepted methods of euthanasia among terminally ill people," brought this action after City refused to issue it a permit to solicit because it did not meet the 75% requirement.

    The case is before the Supreme Court. The Court should declare the ordinance

A. constitutional, because the 75% rule serves a legitimate state interest in preserving the integrity of charities.

B. constitutional, because the right to solicit for a charity is balanced against the interest of the state in preventing fraud and crime.

C. unconstitutional, because the ordinance violates the protections afforded by the First Amendment.

D. constitutional, because the ordinance has as a purpose the protection from undue annoyance and the preservation of residential privacy.

26. The city of Kingco amended its ordinance to require that "adult theatres" (defined in the ordinance) could not be located either within 100 feet of each other or within 500 feet of any residential area. This zoning requirement was passed to protect the residential character of neighborhoods from destruction. American Red-White-and-Blue Movies, Inc., is the owner of two adult theaters. One is a regular theater building located about 1,000 feet from another adult theater. The second theater is a converted gas station which is near another adult theater and adjacent to a residential area, in violation of the zoning ordinance. American has filed this action to have the zoning requirement declared unconstitutional.

The court should hold that

A. the zoning ordinance is in violation of the protections afforded by the First Amendment of the Constitution.

B. the zoning ordinance is invalid because it is a form of spot zoning.

C. the zoning ordinance is valid in that it covers the whole city of Kingco.

D. the zoning ordinance is valid because material protected by the First Amendment is subject to zoning and licensing requirements.

Questions 27—29 are based on the following fact situation:

The state of Aricaltex was suffering a dual problem—that is, an influx of illegal immigrants and high unemployment as a result of a near-depression caused by layoffs in the tourist-service industry. In an attempt to alleviate both problems, the state of Aricaltex enacted a statute providing for the immediate hiring of 100,000 employees to repair, maintain, and otherwise work at the discretion of the Director of Highways. The statute further stated that preference would be given to persons who had worked in the tourist-service industry for five years and had been laid off. Section 2 of the statute provided that resident aliens would be employed only if no employees were available from the tourist-service industry as provided for above.

27. In a challenge to the constitutionality of that part of the statute providing for the hiring of resident aliens on a second-priority basis, which of the following would be most helpful?

   A. The Privileges and Immunities Clause of the Fourteenth Amendment.

   B. The reserved powers of the state under the Tenth Amendment.

   C. The Equal Protection Clause of the Fourteenth Amendment.

   D. The Fourteenth Amendment Due process Clause.

28. In a challenge to the first part of the statute providing for the employment of persons who worked five years for the tourist-service industry and were laid off, which of the following is most relevant?

   A. The Privileges and Immunities Clause of Article IV.

   B. The Equal Protection Clause of the Fourteenth Amendment.

   C. The reserved powers of the state under the Tenth Amendment.

   D. The Privileges and Immunities Clause of the Fourteenth Amendment.

29. Assume, for the purpose of this question only, that the state supreme court of Aricaltex declared the statute to be unconstitutional on the ground that it was in conflict with the Supremacy Clause of the Constitution as well as the Equal Protection Claus of the state constitution. Will the decision be reviewed by the United States Supreme Court?

   A. No, because it does not meet the requirements of certiorari.

   B. Yes, because it meets the requirements of appeal.

C. Yes, because the Supreme Court has original jurisdiction of all cases to which the state is a party.

D. No, because of the "adequate and independent state ground" theory.

30. Ted owned bowling lanes and needed to buy some new bowling balls. On February 1, he read an ad from FMA, a major manufacturer of bowling balls, that they were having a special on balls: 40 balls in various weights and drilled in various sizes for $10 per ball. Ted immediately filled out the order form for the 40 balls and deposited it, properly stamped and addressed, into the mail. The very next day, Ted received in the mail a letter from FMA, sent out as part of their advertising campaign, stating in relevant part that they will sell Ted 40 bowling balls at $10 per ball. On February 3, FMA received Ted's order. On February 4, the balls were shipped.

On what day did an enforceable contract arise?

A. February 1, the day Ted deposited his order in the mail.

B. February 2, the day Ted received the letter from FMA.

C. February 3, the day FMA received Ted's letter.

D. February 4, the day the balls were shipped.

Questions 31—33 are based on the following fact situation:

Mary, 17 years old, was an unemployed disappointment to her parents. To teach Mary to be more self-sufficient, Mary's parents took a one-month trip to Europe, leaving Mary at home to take care of the house. They left Mary $400, which she promptly spent on her first weekend party. By the end of the next week, Mary ran out of food and became hungry. She walked to the local grocery store (the family car was out of gas) and explained her predicament to the manager. He told Mary that if she agreed to work at the store for 20 hours a week for three weeks, she could have $75 worth of groceries. Although it seemed like a lot of work for $75 worth of groceries, Mary needed to eat, and so she accepted, picked up her groceries, promised to report for work the next day, and left.

While on the way home, Mary decided that the idea of credit was not so bad, as for a mere promise she obtained $75 worth of groceries. Just then, she passed Buddy's Budget Autos and decided that she would really impress her parents if she had her own car when they returned. She negotiated with Buddy, the owner of Buddy's, to obtain an $800 car in exchange for her promise to work for Buddy 20 hours a week for eight weeks. When Buddy agreed, they drew up a contract.

While driving home from Buddy's, Mary lost control of the car and crashed into a tree. Both the car and the groceries were completely destroyed. Mary suffered minor injuries. Mary's parents immediately flew home to care for their injured daughter.

31. If the grocery store sues Mary for the cost of the groceries and wins, it will be because

    A. Mary promised to pay for them.

    B. Mary cannot return the groceries so she cannot return the store to the status quo ante.

    C. Mary needed the food.

    D. the contract was not within the Statute of Frauds.

32. If the grocery store sues Mary for the cost of the groceries and loses, it will be because

    A. Mary was a minor.

    B. the groceries were destroyed and thus there was a failure of consideration.

    C. the contract was unconscionable.

    D. it was impossible for Mary to perform.

33. If Buddy sues Mary for the price of the car and loses, it will be because

    A. the contract was unconscionable.

    B. Mary did not need the car.

    C. since the car was destroyed, there is no consideration to support the bargain.

D. the purpose of the contract has been frustrated.

34. On June 15, Homeowner and Carpenter formed a valid oral contract in which Carpenter agreed to construct an extension to Homeowner's home, using materials supplied by Homeowner, in exchange for $2,000. After the work had been completed but before Homeowner had made any payment, Carpenter called Homeowner and instructed him to pay the $2,000 due on the extension work to Woodshop, a creditor of Carpenter's. If Woodshop thereafter brings an action against Homeowner for $2,000, will Woodshop prevail?

    A. Yes, because Woodshop was the intended beneficiary of the original Homeowner-Carpenter contract.

    B. Yes, because there has been a proper assignment.

    C. No, because personal service contracts are not assignable.

    D. No, because Woodshop could not perform the construction work done by Carpenter.

35. Lana was a prominent socialite, noted for her lavish entertainments and her attractiveness. Although Lana was "fortyish," she regularly worked out at her health club and was proud of her mature but youthful figure. She decided to have a nude painting done of herself, and she looked forward to watching people's reactions seeing the painting prominently displayed in her living room. She contracted in writing with artist Pierre. He agreed to paint Lana nude for $10,000. The fee was payable upon the completion of the painting, provided that the painting was to Lana's "complete and utter satisfaction." On the same afternoon that Pierre entered into the contract with Lana he assigned the contract to Taylor. Pierre then painted Lana's picture. After the job was done, Lana told him, "That's a very good likeness of me, but it shows my defects, so I'm not satisfied." Lana refused to accept the painting or pay Pierre or Taylor.

    Can Taylor recover from Lana?

    A. Yes, because the condition in the agreement between Lana and Pierre did not apply to Taylor.

B. Yes, because otherwise an unjust enrichment will occur.

C. No, because rights rising under personal services contracts are not assignable.

D. No, because Lana was not satisfied with the painting.

36. Joni met Jasper in "Singleton's," a tavern catering to young, unattached urban professionals. After exchanging about a half an hour of small talk, Joni told Jasper that she greatly admired the diamond stickpin he had in his lapel. "Oh this," Jasper laughed. "It's no diamond; it's only a piece of glass." Joni acknowledged Jasper's statement, but kept commenting on how nice it looked, and that would go perfectly with her favorite designer business suit. After about a half hour of further conversation, Jasper orally agreed to sell the stickpin to her for $510. It was agreed that on Friday, two days hence, at 6 p.m., Jasper would bring the stickpin to Singleton's and Joni would bring the $510 in cash. Jasper duly appeared with the pin, but Joni failed to appear. Jasper filed suit against Joni for $510.

    Joni's best defense is that

    A. $510 was an unconscionable amount to pay for a piece of glass.

    B. the agreement was not supported by consideration.

    C. the agreement violated the Statute of Frauds.

    D. neither Joni nor Jasper was a merchant.

37. Peter and James inherited Orangeacre as joint tenants from their parents. Only half of the acreage was planted with oranges, and Peter decided that to increase productivity, the balance of the land should be planted with a different variety of oranges.

    James refused to participate in the project, and Peter brought an action for declaratory relief alleging that he was entitled to be reimbursed for half of the cost of the improvement.

    Which of the following correctly describes the result in the action?

    A. Peter will be denied the requested judgment.

B. Peter will be granted the requested judgment.

C. The result depends upon whether James will receive an economic benefit.

D. The result depends upon whether the improvements will produce sufficient income to amortize their cost.

38. Even though Ed Jones and Edith Smith had never formally married, they lived together for 10 years as husband and wife. During this time Edith identified herself as "Mrs. Jones," with the knowledge and consent of Ed. For the entire period, Ed and Edith maintained joint checking accounts and filed joint income tax returns as Mr. and Mrs. Ed Jones. During this period off cohabitation, Ed Jones decided to buy a home. The deed identified the grantee as "Ed Jones and Edith Jones, his wife, and their heirs and assigns forever as tenants by the entirety." Ed made a down payment of $20,000 and executed a mortgage for the unpaid balance. Both he and Edith signed the note for the unpaid balance as husband and wife. Ed continued to make the monthly payments as they became due until he and Edith had an argument and decided to separate. Ed abandoned Edith and the house. Edith then made the payments for six months. At the end of this period, Edith brought an action against Ed for partition of the land in question. Assume that the jurisdiction does not recognize the common law marriage. Assume further that the jurisdiction has no applicable statute on the subject.

Edith's request for partition should be

A. granted, because the estate created by the deed was not a tenancy by the entirety.

B. granted, because the tenancy by the entirety that was created by the deed was severed when Ed abandoned Edith.

C. denied, because a tenant by the entirety has no right to partition.

D. denied, because Ed has absolute title to the property.

39. Billings conveyed Green Acre "To Samuels, his heirs and assigns, so long as the premises are used for agricultural purposes, then to Richards, his heirs and assigns."

    As a consequence of the conveyance, Billings's interest in Green Acre is

    A. a right of entry.

    B. a possibility of reverter.

    C. a fee simple absolute because the conveyance violates the Rule Against Perpetuities.

    D. nothing.

40. Tom leased an apartment from Lon for a period of one year. At the end of the year, Tom continued occupying the apartment, paying Lon the $250 rent in advance each month. Tom had continually complained to Lon about the facilities provided for trash disposal behind the apartment house. Finally, after receiving no response from Lon, Tom complained to the Health Department, who in turn mandated that Lon substantially improve the trash facilities for the apartment building. Shortly thereafter, Lon notified Tom that his rent was being increased to $400 per month. Tom protested and pointed out that all of the other tenants in the apartment building paid rent of $250 per month. Lon then gave Tom the required statutory notice that the tenancy was being terminated at the earliest possible time. By an appropriate action, Tom contested Lon's right to terminate.

    If Tom succeeds, it will be because

    A. the doctrine prohibiting retaliatory eviction is part of the law of the jurisdiction.

    B. a periodic tenancy was created by implication.

    C. a landlord must generally charge the same rent for all units located in one complex.

    D. Lon failed to establish a valid reason why Tom's rent needed to be raised.

41. Employer owned Blackwood in fee simple. Employer was very happy with the service Employee had given him over the years. As a bonus, Employer decided to give Blackwood to Employee. Employer presented a deed conveying Blackwood to Employee. The deed was never recorded. Six months later, Employer found that he was in dire financial straits and needed Blackwood back to complete a sale of the tract of land. He asked Employee to please destroy the deed, which Employee dutifully and voluntarily did. Shortly thereafter, Employer and Employee were killed in an explosion of the factory where they both worked. Each of the successors in interest claimed title to Blackwood.

The probable outcome will be that

A. Employer was the owner of Blackwood, because Employee had voluntarily destroyed the deed.

B. Employer was the owner of Blackwood, because the destruction of the deed by Employee relates back and predates the present transfer of the deed to Employee.

C. Employee was the owner of Blackwood, because the deed was merely evidence of his title and its destruction was insufficient to cause title to pass back to Employer.

D. Employee was the owner of Blackwood, because his destruction of the deed to Blackwood was under the undue influence of Employer.

42. Luke and Linda were not married, but had lived together for two years. As they felt that their relationship was very stable, they decided to leave their leased apartment and purchase a home. Luke and Linda each put up 50% of the down payment on Whiteacre. They took title as tenants in common, and each orally promised the other that the survivor should take title to Whiteacre. Luke and Linda lived at Whiteacre for three years, equitably dividing mortgage payments and maintenance expenses. They were then involved in a serious car accident. Linda was killed almost instantly and Luke died in the hospital one week later. Neither Luke nor

Linda left a will. Linda was survived only by her mother, Meghan. Luke was survived only by his brother, Bobby.

Who owns Whiteacre?

A. Meghan owns the whole.

B. Bobby owns the whole.

C. Meghan and Bobby each have a one-half interest as tenants in common.

D. Meghan and Bobby each have a one-half interest as joint tenants.

Questions 43—44 are based on the following fact situation:

Ophelia wished to install an in-ground swimming pool in her backyard. She hired Acme Pool Company to do the installation. Ophelia chose to locate the pool on the west end of her rather large backyard, close to the property line dividing her yard from her neighbor Norbert's property. She told Norbert that she intended to install the pool, and she told him that, when it was completed, she would invite him and his family to use it.

On the day that Acme began excavation for the pool, Norbert was at home. He stood outside in his backyard to watch the workers to be sure that they did not drive their equipment over his property. The workers wisely kept to Ophelia's property. Unfortunately, when the excavation was nearly completed, subsidence on Norbert's property, caused by the excavation, caused part of Norbert's backyard lawn to collapse. Norbert was understandably upset.

43. If Norbert sues Ophelia for the damage to his lawn, how will a court most likely rule?

    A. For Norbert, because Ophelia is absolutely liable for the damage to Norbert's land.

    B. For Norbert, but only if Ophelia's excavation was negligent.

    C. For Ophelia, because only the lawn was damaged, not any of the buildings located on the property.

    D. For Ophelia, because she had no duty to provide support for Norbert's land.

44. Assume for purposes of this question only that Ophelia's excavation caused Norbert's garage to collapse. What is Ophelia's best defense to an action by Norbert for damage to the garage?

   A. Ophelia gave notice to Norbert of her intention to excavate and he made no objection.

   B. Ophelia had hired Acme based on good recommendations.

   C. Ophelia's excavation was done in a proper manner, and there would have been no subsidence except for the fact that the garage was there.

   D. Norbert's garage was made of solid concrete and thus was unusually heavy.

45. Pacifica Railroad Company had operated freight and passenger service over the line running from Bay City to Metropolis for over 70 years, but the increasing use of autos and planes for passenger travel and trucks for freight forced the railroad to cease all rail service in 1977. A portion of the rail line ran over the westernmost portion of 40 acres of farmland owned by Johnson pursuant to an easement granted by Johnson's predecessors in interest, and subject to which Johnson purchased the land in 1974.

   In 1990, Johnson constructed several large structures for use in housing chickens and began operating a chicken farm, producing eggs and fryers for markets in Bay City. Johnson learned in 1993 that Pacifica intends to institute passenger rail service between Bay City and Metropolis, and he is afraid that the noise and vibration of the passing trains will adversely affect his egg production. He brings an action in state court to quiet title to the area of rail easement and to enjoin Pacifica from entering upon his property. The statutory prescriptive period is 10 years.

   How should the court rule?

   A. For Johnson, because Pacifica has abandoned the easement.

   B. For Johnson, because Pacifica's use of the easement will interfere unreasonably with his egg production.

   C. For Pacifica, because it has not abandoned the easement.

D. For Pacifica, because Johnson's failure to use the land under the easement precludes him from asserting that the easement has been abandoned.

Questions 46—48 are based on the following fact situation:

In the mid-1980s, Sidney entered into a partnership with Jay to develop some land that had been in Sidney's family for many years.

In 1989, in compliance with all applicable laws, and after receiving all necessary permits, the partnership, BayShore Development, began construction on two projects. The first, BayShore Heights, consists of 500 single-family residences built on 250 acres. The second, BayShore Mall, was a shopping center built on 100 acres next to the north end of BayShore Heights.

46. With consideration of likely court enforcement of the following, which method should BayShore Development use to ensure that BayShore Heights retains its residential character?
    A. All deeds should contain negative easements.
    B. All deeds should be subject to conditions subsequent.
    C. All deeds should include covenants.
    D. Ensure the residential character by developing the area in accordance with zoning laws.

47. Immediately to the west of BayShore Heights, Sidney owned additional acreage on which, in 1993, he desired to build another group of 250 single-family homes. To ensure their marketability, Sidney desired to sell them like BayShore Heights homes, and to that extent, intended that the deeds to the new homes contain the same restrictions as those in BayShore Heights and be enforceable in the same manner by owners in both developments. Will Sidney be successful in this plan?
    A. No, zoning restrictions will control.
    B. No, because in order to have such restrictions, the entire project must have been built at the same time.

C. Yes, the restrictions will be equally enforceable for this new project as they were for BayShore Heights.

D. Yes, provided that a court considers this new project to be part of a common development scheme with BayShore Heights.

48. Clay, a developer who wanted to build high-rise condominiums on the remaining acreage owned by Sidney, seeks to purchase the property. Assuming that the condominiums will block the view of the bay of many of the homes in BayShore Heights, what is the effect the original BayShore Heights project many have on Clay's title to this property?

   A. Clay, who received title from Sidney, is restricted from using the property for anything but single-family dwellings.

   B. Clay will be subject to an implied easement for light and air, and the BayShore Heights owners can enjoin the building of high-rise condominiums.

   C. The creation of the original BayShore Heights project gives the owners of those homes a right, enforceable at law, of first refusal to buy the acreage offered to Clay.

   D. Clay takes title free of any claim by the owners of BayShore Heights because the owners have no enforceable claim against Sidney.

Questions 49—50 are based on the following fact situation:

Lou owned Blackacre, a large parcel of land. In 1960, Lou decided to subdivide Blackacre into 20 separate lots. Lou sold Lots 1–19, retaining Lot 20 for himself to live on. The deeds for each of the 19 lots sold by Lou contained the following restriction: "All lots within the Blackacre subdivision shall be used for residential purposes only." The purchasers of Lots 1–19 each built residences on their property. Lou lived on Lot 20 in the Blackacre subdivision until his death, when it was sold without any restrictions to Al. In 1980, Al sold Lot 20 to Neil, without any restrictions. In 1990, Neil decided to build a grocery store on Lot 20. Sherry, an adjoining owner in the

Blackacre subdivision, informed Neil of the restriction and told him that he would be unable to build the grocery store.

49. If the restriction to use the land for residential purposes only is held to apply to Lot 20, it will be because the restriction is

   A. an equitable servitude.

   B. a covenant running with the land.

   C. a reciprocal negative servitude.

   D. part of a general plan.

50. Assume that when Neil purchased Lot 20 from Al in 1980, he was furnished with an abstract of title by Al and was assured by Al that the land was unrestricted. The abstract of title showed that Lot 20 was not restricted. Neil contends that he cannot be bound to the residence restriction, because he had no choice of the restriction when he purchased Lot 20. If Sherry brings suit seeking an injunction against Neil's building of the grocery store, will Neil's contention of lack of notice create a valid defense?

   A. Yes, because Neil had neither actual nor constructive notice of the restriction.

   B. Yes, because he relied on the abstract of title and Al's representation in good faith.

   C. No, because the property owners in the Blackacre subdivision have a right to keep the subdivision in the condition that they want it.

   D. No, because Neil would be charged with notice as a result of the residential character of the Blackacre subdivision.

Questions 51—52 are based on the following fact situation:

Emma was the owner in fee simple of Greenacre, a tract of land. In 1965, Emma conveyed Greenacre to Martha, "for life and then to the first child of Martha's sister, Vera, who shall reach the age of 21." Vera was unmarried and childless in 1965. In 1971, Vera married, and in 1973, Vera gave birth to a son, Oscar. In 1994, Oscar reached the age of 21, and Martha was still alive and living on Greenacre.

51. Oscar now seeks to obtain possession of Greenacre and brings an action in ejectment against Martha. Martha's best defense against Oscar's attempt to eject her is that

    A. Martha's life estate was not subject to termination during her lifetime.

    B. Oscar has no claim to Greenacre, because he was not living at the time of Emma's original conveyance.

    C. a conveyance of Greenacre to Oscar violates the Rule Against Perpetuities.

    D. Oscar's interest, if any, would be that of a contingent remainder, and the contingency is Martha's death.

52. Assume that Martha died before Oscar became 21. Assume also that the jurisdiction has abolished the common law rule of destructibility of contingent remainders. Who would be the owner of Greenacre?

    A. Oscar.

    B. Oscar's court-appointed guardian ad litem.

    C. Emma and her heirs in fee simple.

    D. Emma and her heirs would take the estate until Oscar became 21 years of age.

Questions 53—54 are based on the following fact situation:

Dannay is a 10-year-old, and although his parents make sure he is home by 10 p.m. during the school week, they do not really enforce any sort of curfew on their son during the weekend. One Saturday night, when Danny's parents went to bed at midnight, Danny was still out. About 2 a.m., Danny and two other children were arrested by the police for breaking the windows and causing other damage to Bernadette's antique Cord automobile.

53. In a suit by Bernadette against Danny for the damages he caused to her

automobile, Bernadette should

A. prevail, because Danny, at the age of 10, should have been aware of the consequences of his action.

B. prevail, because Danny deliberately damaged her car.

C. not prevail, because Danny is presumed to be under care of his parents and, therefore, is not legally responsible for his tortuous conduct.

D. not prevail, unless she can show that Danny was mature enough to be aware of the consequences of his action.

54. Assume that the jurisdiction has no statute regarding parental liability. In a suit by Bernadette against Danny's parents for the damages caused to her automobile, Bernadette should

A. prevail, because a minor's parents are vicariously liable anytime the minor commits a tortuous act.

B. prevail, because Danny's parents did not ensure that Danny was home at a reasonable hour.

C. not prevail, unless she can show that Danny's parents were aware that Danny has done this sort of act before.

D. not prevail, because there is no reason to assume that Danny's parents could know that Danny might damage Bernadette's automobile.

Questions 55—56 are based on the following fact situation:

Clara has been having a running battle with her neighbor, Duncan, for several months over the fact that when he operates his ham radio at night, it interferes with her television reception. One night at about 2 a.m., Clara was watching one of her favorite old movies on television when Duncan started transmitting on his radio. Furious that he was again causing her to miss something she wanted to watch on television. Clara decided to fix him by cutting down his radio antenna. She got the ladder from her garage and climbed on top of Duncan's two-story house. However, just as she got to the antenna, her foot slipped and if she had not been able to grab hold of one of the support cables, she would have fallen to the street below. Duncan was unable to hear her cries for help because he was using earphones. Fortunately for Clara, the driver of a passing car, Eldon, saw her hanging from Duncan's roof. Eldon immediately came to her rescue and pulled her back onto the roof. However, as he straightened up after getting Clara back on the roof, he accidentally touched Duncan's antenna and suffered an electric shock. He fell from the roof and suffered severe burns on his back and a broken hip.

55. Eldon sued Clara for the injuries he suffered. Eldon should
    A. not prevail, because he voluntarily assumed the risk of injury.
    B. not prevail, because the rescue of Clara was already over before he was injured.
    C. prevail, because Clara was at fault in slipping from Duncan's roof.
    D. prevail, because Clara may have been killed if she had fallen to the street.

56. Can Eldon assert a valid claim against Duncan for the injuries he suffered while trying to rescue Clara?
    A. Yes, because Duncan's refusal to take steps to insure that his radio would not interfere with Clara's television created this problem.
    B. Yes, if the facts show that Duncan could have taken steps to prevent his antenna from shocking anyone.
    C. No, because Eldon voluntarily assumed the risks.
    D. No, because Duncan was not at fault.

57. Worker entered into a written contract with Owner to install aluminum siding onto Owner's house. The contract called for all work to be completed by the following Tuesday. On that date, Worker finished installing the siding rather late in the afternoon. Wishing to get home as soon as possible, Worker decided that he would come back the next day and pick up his ladder and tools. Worker could not tell Owner of this plan, however, because Owner was out of town overnight on business. During the night, a thief used

Worker's ladder and tools to gain entrance to Owner's home and steal Owner's television set and stereo. Owner had asserted a claim against Worker for damages for the loss of the television and the stereo.

In his claim against Worker, Owner will

A. prevail, because by leaving the ladder and tools out, Worker created the risk that a person might unlawfully enter the house.

B. prevail, because Worker failed to get Owner's permission to leave his ladder and tools on Owner's property overnight.

C. not prevail, because the act of the thief was an independent superseding cause.

D. not prevail, because Owner's only recovery would be by way of an action for breach of contract.

58. A city ordinance required that all dogs be leashed when taken outside of an enclosed area. Bee often allowed her dog, Bop, to run loose in front of Bee's house. One day, when Bop was running loose, Dina was driving her car up the street in front of Bee's house. The day was clear and sunny and Dina was driving carefully at a speed somewhat below the posted limit. Bop dashed out into the street from between two parked cars. Dina alertly applied her brakes, but could not avoid striking Bop. Pris, driving another vehicle behind Dina, promptly applied her brakes as soon as she saw the red lights glow on the rear of Dina's vehicle. However, Pris' vehicle struck the rear of Dina's vehicle. Both of the vehicles suffered damage and both drivers suffered minor injuries which required X-rays and other medical attention.

If Pris sues Dina for her vehicle damage and personal injuries, Pris will

A. prevail, because the ordinance was designed to prevent dogs from being hit by cars.

B. prevail, because Dina was a proximate cause of the accident.

C. not prevail, because Dina obeyed the traffic laws.

D. not prevail, unless Dina herself was negligent.

59. Parker was enjoying a steak in a local restaurant when he started to choke. A waiter saw that Dr. Macmillan was sitting at a nearby table, and the waiter ran over to ask her to help him save Parker. Dr. Macmillan stood up and told the waiter that she did not want to become involved, and she left the restaurant. Soon afterwards, the paramedics arrived and they were able to save Parker's life. Unfortunately, he suffered brain damage due to lack of oxygen.

    Parker brings a suit against Dr. Macmillan seeking damages for his injuries. Parker's medical expert testified that had Parker received prompt medical attention there would have been no injuries at all. Can Parker recover damages from Dr. Macmillan?

    A. Yes, if the jurisdiction in which this accident occurred had a statute relieving doctors from malpractice claims when they give emergency first aid.

    B. Yes, if a reasonable doctor in Dr. Macmillan's position would have rendered first aid.

    C. No, because Dr. Macmillan was not responsible for Parker's condition.

    D. No, unless it can be shown that Dr. Macmillan knew that Parker was substantially certain to suffer injury unless he received medical assistance from a doctor.

60. Paine and Duncan were playing tennis. Duncan became highly irritated because every time Duncan prepared to serve, Paine started talking loudly. Paine's loud talk distracted Duncan from his game, and Duncan usually faulted on his serves. Duncan told Paine to "cut it out," but Paine persisted in the behavior.

    Standing several feet away, Duncan swung his tennis racket toward Paine's head. However, Duncan slipped as he swung the racket and it flew out of his hand as he lost his balance. The racket flew through the air and struck Paine in the head.

附录一
2018年11月法律英语证书（LEC）全国统一考试试题及参考答案

Has Paine grounds for a battery action against Duncan?

A. Yes, if Duncan intended to create a reasonable apprehension in Paine.

B. Yes, because the racket struck Paine.

C. No, because Duncan did not intend the racket to strike Paine.

D. No, but only if Duncan can prove that the owner of the tennis court had not maintained the court properly and this caused Duncan to slip.

61. A homeowner was using a six-foot stepladder to clean the furnace in his home. The homeowner broke his arm when he slipped and fell from the ladder. The furnace had no warnings or instructions on how it was to be cleaned.

    In a suit by the homeowner against the manufacture of the furnace to recover for his injury, is the homeowner likely to prevail?

    A. No, because the danger of falling from a ladder is obvious.

    B. No, because the homeowner should have hired a professional to clean the furnace.

    C. Yes, because the furnace did not have a ladder attached to it for cleaning purpose.

    D. Yes, because the lack of warnings or instructions for how to clean the furnace made the furnace defective.

62. A college student was asleep in his bed in a college dormitory when his roommate, in a drunken fury, entered their room intending to attack the student with an ice pick. Fortunately, the phone rang and awakened the student. The roommate retreated quickly and threw the ice pick under his own bed in the same room. The next day, the student heard from friends about the roommate's murderous plans and later found the ice pick under the roommate's bed. Even though the college expelled his roommate, the student remained extremely upset and afraid to sleep.

    In a suit against the roommate for assault, will the student prevail?

    A. No, because the roommate did not touch the student.

    B. No, because the student was not awake when the roommate entered the room and was unaware until later that the roommate was intending to attack him.

C. Yes, because it was reasonable for the student to feel afraid of sleeping in his room afterward.

D. Yes, because the roommate intended to inflict serious harm.

63. When a tire of a motorist's car suffered a blowout, the car rolled over and the motorist was badly injured. Vehicles made by the manufacturer of the motorist's car have been found to be negligently designed, making them dangerously prone to rolling over when they suffer blowouts. A truck driver who was driving behind the motorist when the accident occurred stopped to help. Rescue vehicles promptly arrived, and the truck driver walked along the side of the road to return to his truck. As he approached his truck, he was struck and injured by a speeding car. The truck driver has sued the manufacturer of the injured motorist's car.

Is the truck driver likely to prevail in a suit against the car manufacturer?

A. No, because the car manufacturer's negligence was not the proximate cause of the truck driver's injuries.

B. No, because the truck driver assumed the risk of injury when he undertook to help the motorist.

C. Yes, because it is foreseeable that injuries can result from rollovers.

D. Yes, because the car manufacturer's negligence caused the dangerous situation that invited the rescue by the truck driver.

64. A gas company built a large refining facility that conformed to zoning requirements on land near a landowner's property. The landowner had his own home and a minigolf business on his property.

In a nuisance action against the gas company, the landowner established that the refinery emitted fumes that made many people feel quite sick when they were outside on his property for longer than a few minutes. The landowner's minigolf business had greatly declined as a consequence, and the value of his property had gone down markedly.

Is the owner likely to prevail?

A. No, because the landowner has offered no evidence demonstrating that the gas company was negligent.

B. No, because the refinery comforts to the zoning requirements.

C. Yes, because the refinery has substantially and unreasonably interfered with the landowner's use and enjoyment of his property.

D. Yes, because the value of the landowner's property has declined.

65. A fire that started in the defendant's warehouse spread to the plaintiff's adjacent warehouse. The defendant did not intentionally start the fire, and the plaintiff can produce no evidence as to how the fire started. However, the defendant had failed to install a sprinkle system, which was required by a criminal statute. The plaintiff can produce evidence that had the sprinkle system been installed, it could have extinguished the fire before it spread.

In an action by the plaintiff against the defendant to recover for the fire damage, is it possible for the plaintiff to prevail?

A. No, because the statute provides only for criminal penalties.

B. No, because there is no evidence that the defendant negligently caused the fire to start.

C. Yes, because a landowner is strictly liable for harm to others caused by the spread of fire from his premises under the doctrine of **Rylands v. Fletcher**.

D. Yes, because the plaintiff was harmed as a result of the defendant's violation of a statute that was meant to protect against this type of occurrence.

66. A patent is by nature a monopoly, but it may deserve protection because

A. it is the creation from the inventor's mind, and naturally it should belong to the inventor.

B. the invention may be of great value which will be lost in free and unfettered competition.

C. the overall social benefits outweigh the economic evils in protecting the invention.

D. everyone else in the world is free to come up with his own fresh ideas on development of technology.

67. The patent law in the United States does not specify what subject matters are excluded from patent protection, but courts have carved out certain categories that are not patent-eligible, such as

   A. computer programs.

   B. business methods.

   C. bacteria.

   D. abstract ideas.

68. A, being the inventor of an extremely viable invention that works a tremendous commercial success, formed a company of his own and assigned all his patents to the company. Later, bad blood developed between him and his associates in the company, and he resigned. He now files a request with the Patent Office to invalidate those patents held by the company. He would be stopped from doing so under

   A. Assignor Estoppel.

   B. Licensee Estoppel.

   C. Equitable Estoppel.

   D. Collateral Estoppel.

69. In intellectual property cases, an injunction (i.e., a court order of cease and desist from present business activities), either temporary or permanent, is a very harsh measure that could work tremendous economic difficulties for a defendant. When allowing such a measure, the court should usually consider all of the following factors *EXCEPT*:

   A. that the plaintiff has won previous cases on the same or similar claims of the patent.

   B. that the defendant is a multimillion dollar international conglomerate.

C. that the plaintiff will be injured by the irreparable harms resulting from the alleged infringing activities.

D. that more and more potential infringers will follow if the present one at suit is not stopped.

70. A trademark may tend to become a generic mark when it is used

   A. as a noun extensively for a product.

   B. as an adjective describing a product.

   C. as a noun indicating the source of a product.

   D. as an adverb strengthening the effect of an adjective.

71. An executive of an accounting firm was fired and told to leave the firm. The executive went home, but she returned that night to retrieve her key. She could no longer open the door to the building, and she forced the door open and went to her former office. To avoid attracting attention, she did not turn on any lights. In the dark, she knew that she was taking some items that were not hers; she planned to sort these out later and return them.

   Upon arriving home, she found that she had taken a record book and some financial papers that belonged to the firm. After thinking it over and becoming angrier over being fired, she burned the book and papers in her fireplace.

   The jurisdiction has expanded the crime of burglary to include all buildings. What crime(s) has the executive committed?

   A. Burglary and larceny.

   B. Burglary, but not larceny.

   C. Larceny, but not burglary.

   D. Neither larceny nor burglary.

72. A woman and her sister took a trip to the Caribbean. When they passed through U.S. Customs inspection upon their return, the customs officials found liquid cocaine in several bottles each of them was carrying. They

were arrested. Upon separate questioning by customs officers, the woman broke down and cried, "I told my sister there were too many officers at this airport." The sister did not give a statement.

The woman and her sister were indicted for conspiracy to import cocaine. They were tried separately. At the woman's trial, after the government introduced evidence and rested its case, her lawyer moved for a judgment of acquittal on grounds of insufficient evidence.

Should the court grant the motion?

A. No, because the evidence shows that both the woman and her sister agreed to import cocaine.

B. No, because the evidence shows that both the woman and her sister possessed cocaine.

C. Yes, because the evidence shows that only the woman possessed cocaine.

D. Yes, because the evidence shows that the woman cooperated by giving a statement.

73. A man and his friend were watching a televised football game at the man's home. Upset by a penalty called by the referee, the friend threw a bottle of beer at the man's television, breaking the screen. Enraged, the man picked up a nearby hammer and hit the friend on the head with it. The friend died from the blow.

The crimes below are listed in descending order of seriousness.

In a jurisdiction that follows common law principles, what is the most serious crime of which the man could properly be convicted?

A. Murder.

B. Voluntary manslaughter.

C. Involuntary manslaughter.

D. Assault.

74. A man had spent the evening drinking at a local bar and was weaving down the street on his way home, singing. Suddenly, a person wearing a

cartoon character mask jumped out from an alley, pointed his gun at the man, and snarled, "This is loaded, buddy, and I don't mind using. Hand over your cash pronto!" The man failed to understand what was going on and started to howl with laughter at the sight of the cartoon mask. Surprised and rattled by the man's reaction, the masked gunman fled. The man soon recovered his composure and stagger home safely.

The crimes below are listed in descending order of seriousness.

What is the most crime of which the masked gunman may properly be charged and convicted?

A. Attempted robbery.

B. Attempted battery.

C. Attempted larceny.

D. No crime.

75. A defendant was charged with battery, defined as at common law. At trial, an expert witness testified for the defense that the defendant, an athlete, was under the influence of a performance-enhancing drug at the time he committed the battery and that he would not have done so had he not been influenced. The defendant asked for an instruction to the effect that if the jury believed that he was influenced by the drug at the time of the crime and would not have committed it otherwise, it had to acquit him.

Which of the following circumstances would most aid the defendant's argument in favor of such an instruction?

A. Evidence that the defendant is addicted to this drug and has an overwhelming urge to consume it.

B. Evidence that the defendant's coach, who gave him the drug, told him it was only an aspirin.

C. Evidence that the victim of the assault taunted the defendant about his use of the drug immediately before the assault.

D. Expert testimony that a reasonable person, on consuming this drug, may experience uncontrollable rages.

76. A common law jurisdiction defines first-degree murder as any murder that is (1) committed by means of poison or (2) premeditated. All other murder is second-degree murder, and manslaughter is defined as at common law.

    An employee was angry with her boss for denying her a raise. Intending to cause her boss discomfort, the employee secretly dropped into his coffee three over-the-counter laxative pills. The boss drank the coffee containing the pills. Although the pills would not have been dangerous to an ordinary person, because the boss was already taking other medication, he suffered a seizure and died.

    If the employee is charged with murder in the first degree, should she be convicted?

    A. Yes, only because she used poison.

    B. Yes, only because she acted with premeditation.

    C. Yes, both because she used poison and because she acted with premeditation.

    D. No.

77. A man asked his girlfriend to lend him something he could use to break into his neighbor's padlocked storage shed in order to steal a lawn mower. She handed him a crowbar. He took the crowbar but then found a bolt cutter that the neighbor had left outside the shed. Using the bolt cutter, he cut the padlock on the shed and took the mower, which he then used to mow his girlfriend's lawn. She was surprised and pleased by this gesture.

    Burglary in the jurisdiction applies to any structure or building, and there is no nighttime element.

    The girlfriend has been charged as an accomplice to burglary and larceny. Of which crimes, if any, is she guilty?

    A. Burglary and larceny.

    B. Burglary, but not larceny, because she intended to assist only in the breaking.

C. Larceny, but not burglary, because she provided no actual assistance to the breaking but received a benefit from the larceny.

D. Neither burglary nor larceny, because she provided no actual assistance.

78. A defendant was tried for armed robbery. The state introduced evidence that a man, identified by witnesses as the defendant, entered a convenience store at 11 p.m. on March 5, threatened the clerk with a gun, and took $75 from the cash register.

    The defendant did not testify but his sister did. She testified that on March 5, at the time of the robbery, the defendant was with her in a city 300 miles away. On cross-examination, the sister admitted having given a statement to the police in which she had said that the defendant was not with her on March 5, but she claimed that the earlier statement was mistaken.

    The court instructed the jury that in order to convict the defendant, they had to find all of the elements of the crime beyond a reasonable doubt.

    As to the defendant's claim of alibi, which of the following additional instructions would be proper?

    A. Alibi is a matter of defense and so must be established by the defendant; however, the burden of persuasion is by a preponderance of the evidence, not beyond a reasonable doubt.

    B. Before you may consider the defendant's claim of alibi, you must decide whether he has produced sufficient evidence to raise the issue.

    C. If you have a reasonable doubt as to whether the defendant was present at the convenience store at about 11p. m. on March 5, you must find him not guilty.

    D. If the defendant's evidence has caused you to have a reasonable doubt as to whether he was the robber, you must find him not guilty.

79. A state statute provides: "Aggravated robbery of the elderly consists of robbery committed against a victim who is 65 years of age or older." Another state statute provides that when a criminal statute does not designate a

necessary mental state, the mental state required is recklessness. A third state statute provides that a person acts recklessly if the person "consciously disregards a substantial and unjustified risk that the material element exists or will result from the persons conduct."

The evidence at a criminal trial showed that the defendant robbed a 66-year-old man outside a senior citizens center. The defendant testified truthfully that the robbery had occurred on a dark night, that she had no idea how old the victim was and had not cared how old the victim was, and that she had intended to rob whomever she encountered. Could the defendant be properly convicted of aggravated robbery of the elderly?

A. No, because the only evidence on the issue showed that the defendant did not know, nor could she reasonably have known, the victim's age.

B. No, because there was no evidence of a substantial risk that the victim was aged 65 or older.

C. Yes, because the evidence was clear that the victim was 66 years old, and the statute is designed to protect the elderly.

D. Yes, because the jury could find that there was no justification for the defendant's conduct and that she was willing to take the risk that the victim was aged 65 or older.

80. While on their way home from a ball game, a driver and his passenger stopped at an all-night gas station. The passenger offered to pay for the gas. While the passenger pumped gas, he was surprised to see the driver enter the station, take money from the unattended cash drawer, and get back in the car. The passenger paid the attendant for the gas, and the driver drove off. The driver offered to reimburse the passenger for the gas, but the passenger declined. After discovering the missing cash, the gas station attendant called the police, and the driver was later stopped. The driver escaped with the stolen money, however, and was never prosecuted. If the passenger is prosecuted for theft as an accomplice, should he be convicted?

A. No, because he had no intent to promote the commission of the offense.

B. No, because the driver, the principal, was never prosecuted.

C. Yes, because he facilitated commission of the offense by failing to make any effort to stop it.

D. Yes, because he paid the attendant while he knew the driver was holding the stolen money.

81. A defendant is being tried for the murder of a woman who disappeared 10 years ago and has not been heard from since. Her body has never been found. The prosecutor has presented strong circumstance evidence that she was murdered by the defendant. To help establish the act of her death, the prosecutor has requested that the judge give the following instruction, based on a recognized presumption in the jurisdiction: "A person missing and not heard from in the last seven years shall be presumed to be deceased."
Is the instruction proper?

A. No, because the fact that someone has not been heard from in seven years does not necessarily lead to a conclusion that the person is dead.

B. No, because mandatory presumptions are not allowed against a criminal defendant on an element of the charged crime.

C. Yes, because it expresses a rational conclusion that the jury should be required to accept.

D. Yes, because the defendant has a chance to rebut the presumption by offering evidence that the woman is alive or has been head from in the last seven years.

82. Several defendants, senior executives of a corporation, were charged with securities fraud. The government called as a witness another executive of the corporation, who had not been charged and who had been given immunity from prosecution, to authenticate handwritten notes that she had made after meetings of the corporation's management team at which the alleged fraud was discussed. The witness testified that she had prepared the notes on her own initiative to help her remember what had happened at the meetings. After this testimony, the government offered the notes

into evidence to establish what had happened at the meetings.

Should the witness's notes be admitted?

A. No, because the notes are hearsay not within any exception.

B. No, because the witness's immunity agreement with the government makes her notes untrustworthy and thus substantially more prejudicial than probative.

C. Yes, because they are business records.

D. Yes, because they are past recollections recorded.

83. A plaintiff sued a defendant, alleging that she was seriously injured when the defendant ran a red light and struck her while she was walking in a crosswalk. During the defendant's case, a witness testified that the plaintiff had told him that she was "barely touched" by the defendant's car.

On cross-examination, should the court allow the plaintiff to elicit from the witness the fact that he is an adjuster for the defendant's insurance company?

A. No, because testimony about liability insurance is barred by the rules of evidence.

B. No, because the reference to insurance raises a collateral issue.

C. Yes, for both substantive and impeachment purposes.

D. Yes, for impeachment purposes only.

84. A defendant was charged with the crime of defrauding the federal agency where he worked as an accountant. At trial, the court allowed the defendant to call his supervisor at the large corporation where he had previously worked, who testified about the defendant's good reputation in the community for honesty. Over objection, the defendant then sought to elicit testimony from his former supervisor that on several occasions the corporation had, without incident, entrusted him with large sums of money.

Should the testimony be admitted?

A. No, because the testimony is extrinsic evidence on a collateral matter.

B. No, because good character cannot be proved by specific instances of conduct unless character is an essential element of the charge or defense.

C. Yes, because it is evidence of a pertinent character trait offered by an accused.

D. Yes, because it is relevant to whether the defendant was likely to have taken money as charged in this case.

85. A plaintiff sued his insurance company for the proceeds of a casualty insurance policy covering his 60-foot yacht, claiming that the yacht was destroyed by an accidental fire. The company denied liability, claiming that the plaintiff hired his friend to set the fire. In the hospital the day after the fire, the friend who had been badly burned in the fire, said to his wife, in the presence of an attending nurse, "I was paid to set the fire." Two weeks later, the friend died of an infection resulting from the burns. At trial, the insurance company called the wife to testify to the friend's statement.

Is the wife's testimony admissible over the plaintiff's objection?

A. No, because the marital privilege survives the communicating spouse's death.

B. No, because the statement was made after the conspiracy ended.

C. Yes, because it is a statement against interest.

D. Yes, because it is a statement by a co-conspirator.

86. A defendant was charged with possession of marijuana with intent to distribute. On direct examination, the defendant testified that he worked with disadvantaged children as a drug counselor, that he hated drugs, that he would "never possess or distribute drugs," and that he had never used drugs and would not touch them. The government offered as a rebuttal witness a police officer who would testify that, three years earlier, he saw the defendant buy cocaine from a street dealer. The defendant objected.

Is the testimony of the police officer about the prior drug transaction admissible to impeach the defendant?

A. No, because the bad act of buying drugs is not sufficiently probative of a witness's character for truthfulness.

B. No, because it is contradiction on a collateral matter.

C. Yes, because it is proper contradiction.

D. Yes, because the bad act shows a disregard for the law and makes it less likely that the defendant would respect the oath of truthfulness.

87. A woman sued her friend for injuries she received as a passenger in the friend's car. On direct examination, the woman testified that the friend had been speeding and ran a red light. On cross-examination, the woman was asked whether she was under the influence of drugs at the time of the accident. The woman invoked the privilege against self-incrimination.

    How should the court treat the woman's claim of privilege?

    A. Deny it, because the woman waived the privilege by voluntarily testifying.

    B. Deny it, because evidence of the woman's drug intoxication is essential to assessing the accuracy of her observations.

    C. Uphold it, because the privilege applies in both civil and criminal cases.

    D. Uphold it, because the woman's credibility impeached by a crime for which she has convicted cannot be not been convicted.

88. A consumer has sued the manufacturer of a microwave oven for burn injuries allegedly caused by the manufacturer's negligent failure to warn purchasers of the dangers of heating foods in certain types of containers. The consumer has offered into evidence three letters, all received by the manufacturer before the oven was shipped to the consumer, in which customers had complained of serious burns under circumstances similar to those in the consumer's case. The manufacturer has objected to the letters on the grounds of hearsay and, in the alternative, has asked for a limiting instruction directing that the letters be considered not for the

truth of the assertions contained in them but only regarding the issue of notice.

How should the court respond?

A. The court should sustain the objection and treat the request for a limiting instruction as moot.

B. The court should overrule the objection and deny the request for a limiting instruction.

C. The court should overrule the objection and give the limiting instruction.

D. The court should overrule the objection but allow only that the letters be read to the jury, not received as exhibits.

89. A plaintiff sued for injuries arising from a car accident, claiming a back injury. At trial, she wished to testify that prior to the accident she had never had any problems with her back.

Is the plaintiff's proposed testimony admissible?

A. No, because the plaintiff has not been qualified as an expert.

B. No, because the plaintiff's pain could have been caused by factors arising after the accident, such as an injure at work.

C. Yes, because it is probative evidence of the plaintiff's injury.

D. Yes, because the testimony of parties is not subject to the lay opinion rule.

90. A plaintiff, who had been injured in an automobile collision with the defendant, sued the defendant for damages. The defendant denied negligence and denied that the plaintiff's injuries were severe. At trial, the plaintiff has offered in evidence a color photograph of himself made from a videotape taken by a television news crew at the scene of the collision. The plaintiff has demonstrated that the videotape has since been routinely reused by the television station and that the footage of the plaintiff was erased. The photograph shows the plaintiff moments after the collision, with his bloodied head protruding at a grotesque angle through the broken windshield of his car.

Should the photograph be admitted over the defendant's objection?

A. No, because the plaintiff has failed to establish that a duplicate could not be found.

B. No, because the plaintiff has failed to produce the original videotape or a duplicate.

C. Yes, because it tends to prove a controverted fact.

D. Yes, because a photograph that establishes a disputed fact cannot be excluded as prejudicial.

91. Before putting her home up for sale, a homeowner painted the living room ceiling to conceal major water damage caused by a leaking roof that had not yet been repaired. On the first day the home was offered for sale, the homeowner gave a buyer a personal tour. The homeowner made no statements at all regarding the water damage or the roof. Without discovering the water damage or the leaking roof and without consulting a lawyer, the buyer immediately agreed in writing to buy the home for $200,000.

Before the closing date, the buyer discovered the water damage and the leaking roof. The cost of repair was estimated mated at $22,000. The buyer has refused to go through with the purchase.

If the homeowner sues the buyer for breach of contract is the homeowner likely to prevail?

A. No, because no contract was formed since the buyer did not have a real opportunity to understand the essential terms of the contract.

B. No, because the homeowner concealed evidence of the water damage and of the leaking roof.

C. Yes, because the homeowner made no affirmative statements of fact about the water damage or the leaking roof.

D. Yes, because the buyer acted unreasonably by failing to employ an inspector to conduct an independent inspection of the home.

92. An engineer entered into a written contract with an owner to serve in the essential position of on-site supervisor for construction of an office building. The day after signing the contract, the engineer was injured while bicycling and was rendered physically incapable of performing as the on-site supervisor for the same pay as originally agreed to by the parties.

   Is the owner likely to prevail in an action against the engineer for damages resulting from his failure to perform under the contract?

   A. No, because the engineer offered a reasonable substitute by offering to serve as an off-site consultant.

   B. No, because the engineer's physical ability can soon recover to perform the contract.

   C. Yes, because the engineer breached the contract by disappointing the owner's expectations.

   D. Yes, because the engineer's duty to perform was personal and absolute.

93. An experienced rancher contracted to harvest his neighbor's wheat crop for S1,000 "when the crop [was] ripe." In early September, the neighbor told the rancher that the crop was ripe. The rancher delayed the harvesting because he had other customers to attend to. The neighbor was concerned that the delay might cause the loss of the crop, for hailstorms were common in that part of the country in the fall. In fact, in early October, before the crop was harvested, it was destroyed by a hailstorm.

   Is the rancher liable for the loss?

   A. No, because no time for performance was established in the contract.

   B. No, because the neighbor failed to tell the rancher that the crop might be destroyed by a hailstorm.

   C. Yes, because at the time the contract was made, the rancher had reason to foresee the loss as a probable result of his breach.

   D. Yes, because a party who undertakes a contractual obligation is liable for all the consequences that flow from his breach.

94. A niece had worked in her aunt's bookstore for many years. The bookstore business, which was housed in a building that the aunt leased, was independently appraised at $200,000. The aunt decided to retire. She wrote to the niece, expressing her affection for the niece and offering to sell her the bookstore business for $125,000 if the landlord would agree to a transfer of the lease. The letter also specified when the aunt would transfer the business. The niece wrote back accepting her aunts offer. In a phone call to the niece, the aunt stated that the landlord had approved attorney to draft a written contract so that there would be a record of the terms. Before the attorney had finished drafting the document, the aunt changed her mind about selling the business and informed the niece of her decision.

In an action for breach of contract brought by the niece against her aunt, is the niece likely to prevail?

A. No, because the motivation for the transfer of the business was the aunt's affection for her niece, not the price.

B. No, because the promised consideration was inadequate in light of the market value of the business.

C. Yes, because the condition concerning the landlord's assent to the transfer of the lease was beyond the control of either party.

D. Yes, because the document being drafted by the attorney was merely a record of an agreement already made, not a condition to it.

95. An actor straight out of drama school and an agent entered into a one-year written contract that described the services the agent would provide. Because he was eager for work, the actor agreed, in the contract, to pay the agent 15 percent of his yearly earnings. At the end of the year, the actor was so pleased with his many roles that he gave the agent 20 percent of his earnings. After the first contract had expired, the actor and the agent decided to continue working together. They photocopied their old contract, changed the date, and signed it. At the end of the year, a dispute arose as to what percentage of earnings the actor owed to the agent. It is

a trade practice in the acting profession for actors to pay their agents 10 percent of their yearly earnings, payable at the end of the year.

What percentage of the actor's earnings is a court most likely to award the agent?

A. 20 percent, because course of dealing is given greater weight than trade usage.

B. 15 percent, because it was an express term of the contract.

C. 10 percent, because trade usage is the applicable default rule.

D. Nothing, because the contract is too indefinite.

Questions 96—100 are logical reasoning test.

96. Acme brand aspirin claims to be the best headache relief available on the market today. To prove this claim, Acme called 10 people and asked them their thoughts on headache relief products. All 10 of them stated that they unequivocally use Acme brand aspirin on a regular basis and that they believe it to be the best headache relief available on the market today.

Which of the following would most weaken this argument?

A. Acme brand aspirin is highly addictive.

B. The 10 people called were spouses of Acme employees.

C. Most people choose to suffer silently through their headaches and take no medicines whatsoever.

D. The 10 people called own stock in a competing company.

97. In order to combat Carville's rampant homeless problem, Mayor Bloomfield recently proposed a ban on sleeping outdoors in the city's many parks. He claims that such a measure will force the homeless to either leave Carville or to find means other than sleeping in public parks.

Which of the following, if true, suggests that Mayor Bloomfield's plan will be successful?

A. Until the ban, the city's many homeless shelters were at less than fifty percent occupancy.

B. Many homeless tend to congregate underneath Carville's numerous overpasses.

C. Adjacent cities have even tougher measures on the homeless sleeping outdoors.

D. The percent of Carville's population that has been homeless has been slowly decreasing in the last five years.

98. Many environmentalists rank global warming as the most serious current threat to the world's environment, citing evidence that over the past 30 years, the global temperature has risen an average of 2 degrees. However, the average global temperature this year is equal to the average global temperature of last year. Global warming, therefore, is not as serious a problem as these environmentalists claim.

The argument is most vulnerable to the criticism in that it

A. argues that because a threat is present, that threat must be more serious than any other possible threat.

B. concludes that because there is lack of evidence for a problem, that problem does not exist.

C. attempts to refute a conclusion about a general trend by appealing to a single counterexample, even though such a counterexample may be consistent with the general trend.

D. relies on the ambiguous use of a key term.

99. Home alarm systems are commonly regarded by insurance companies as improving the safety of the home. However, statistics show that the break-in rate for homes equipped with such alarms is slightly higher than the break-in rate for houses without such alarms.

Which of the following statements, if true, would most help to reconcile the insurance companies' belief with the statistics cited?

A. Home alarm systems are generally installed only in those homes that are in theft-prone areas.

B. Because home alarm systems generate many false alarms, authorities are slow to respond to such alarms.

C. Without signs announcing the presence of a home alarm system, the system does little to deter theft.

D. Home alarm systems offer little protection against practiced thieves.

100. Some people interpret the phrase "survival of the fittest" as "survival of the strongest." However, inasmuch as "strong" is interpreted as "superior in physical size and prowess", this is incorrect. Although strength and size provide a survival advantage within a species in such tasks as breeding, fighting for food, and running from predators, a species will survive only if its overall resource requirement for maintaining its strength does not outweigh the resources available, as is often the case during a famine or other ecological disaster.

Based on the passage above, which of the following statements must be true?

A. If a species' resource requirement for maintaining its strength outweighs the resources available, that species will not survive.

B. Strength does not provide a survival advantage for hunting food.

C. The phrase "survival of the fittest" should not be used by the scientific community.

D. The species with the least strength is the most likely to survive in a famine.

法律英语证书（LEC）全国统一考试
考试大纲

试 卷 二

提示：本试卷为阅读、翻译、写作题。请将各题答案书写在答题纸的对应位置上，勿在卷面上直接作答。

Part I. Case Reading and Comprehension (25 points)
Read the case carefully and briefly answer the questions following the case.

HOUSE OF LORDS
Date: 17 July 1868
Between:
JOHN RYLANDS AND JEHU HORROCKS PLAINTIFF
– v –
THOMAS FLETCHER DEFENDANTS

THE LORD CHANCELLOR (Lord *Cairns*):

My Lords, in this case the Plaintiff (I may use the description of the parties in the action) is the occupier of a mine and works under a close of land. The Defendants are the owners of a mill in his neighbourhood, and they proposed to make a reservoir for the purpose of keeping and storing water to be used about their mill upon another close of land, which, for the purposes of this case, may be taken as being adjoining to the close of the Plaintiff, although, in point of fact, some intervening land lay between the two. Underneath the close of land of the Defendants on which they proposed to construct their reservoir there were certain old and disused mining passages and works. There were five vertical shafts, and some horizontal shafts communicating with them. The vertical shafts had been filled up with soil and rubbish, and it does not appear that any person was aware of the existence either of the vertical shafts or of the horizontal works communicating with them. In the course of the working by the Plaintiff of his mine, he had gradually worked through the seams of coal underneath the close, and had come into contact with the old and disused works underneath the close of the Defendants.

Under these circumstances the reservoir of the Defendants was constructed. It was constructed by them through the agency and under the inspection of an engineer and a contractor. Personally, the Defendants appear to have taken no part in the works, or to have been aware of any want of security connected with them. As regards the engineer and the contractor, we must take it from the case that they did not exercise, as far as they were concerned, that reasonable care and caution which they might have exercised, taking notice, as they appear to have taken notice, of the vertical shafts filled up in the manner which I have mentioned. However, my Lords, when the reservoir was constructed, and filled, or partly filled, with water, the weight of the water bearing upon the disused and imperfectly filled-up vertical shafts, broke through those shafts. The water passed down them and into the horizontal workings, and from the horizontal workings under the close of the Defendants it passed on into the workings under the close of the Plaintiff, and flooded his mine, causing considerable damage, for which this action was brought.

The Court of Exchequer, when the special case stating the facts to which I have referred, was argued, was of opinion that the Plaintiff had established no cause of action. The Court of Exchequer Chamber, before which an appeal from this judgment was argued, was of a contrary opinion, and the Judges there unanimously arrived at the conclusion that there was a cause of action, and that the Plaintiff was entitled to damages.

My Lords, the principles on which this case must be determined appear to me to be extremely simple. The Defendants, treating them as the owners or occupiers of the close on which the reservoir was constructed, might lawfully have used that close for any purpose for which it might in the ordinary course of the enjoyment of land be used; and if, in what I may term the natural user of that land, there had been any accumulation of water, either on the surface or underground, and if, by the operation of the laws of nature, that accumulation of water had passed off into the close occupied by the Plaintiff, the Plaintiff could not have complained that that result had taken place. If he had desired to guard himself against it, it would have lain upon him to have done so, by leaving, or by interposing, some barrier between his close and the close of the Defendants in order to have prevented that operation of the laws of nature.

As an illustration of that principle, I may refer to a case which was cited in the argument before your Lordships, the case of **Smith v. Kenrick (7 C. B. 515.)** in the Court of Common Pleas.

On the other hand if the Defendants, not stopping at the natural use of their close, had desired to use it for any purpose which I may term a non-natural use, for the purpose of introducing into the close that which in its natural condition was not in or upon it, for the purpose of introducing water either above or below ground in quantities and in a manner not the result of any work or operation on or under the land, and if in consequence of their doing so, or in consequence of any imperfection in the mode of their doing so, the water came to escape and to pass off into the close of the Plaintiff, then it appears to me that that which the Defendants were doing they were doing at their own peril; and, if in the course of their doing it, the evil arose to which I have referred, the evil, namely, of the escape of the water and its passing away to the close of the Plaintiff and injuring the Plaintiff, then for the consequence of that, in my opinion, the Defendants would be liable. As the case of Smith v. Kenrick is an illustration of the first principle to which I have referred, so the second principle to which I have referred is well illustrated by another case in the same Court, the case of *Baird v. Williamson (15 C. B.(N. S.) 317.)*, which was also cited in the argument at the Bar.

My Lords, these simple principles, if they are well founded, as it appears to me they are, really dispose of this case.

The same result is arrived at on the principles referred to by Mr. Justice *Blackburn* in his judgment, in the Court of Exchequer Chamber, where he states the opinion of that Court as to the law in these words: "We think that the true rule of law is, that the person who, for his own purposes, brings on his land and collects and keeps there anything likely to do mischief if it escapes, must keep it in at his peril; and if he does not do so, is *primâ facie* answerable for all the damage which is the natural consequence of its escape. He can excuse himself by showing that the escape was owing to the Plaintiff's default; or, perhaps, that the escape was the consequence of *vis major*, or the act of God; but as nothing of this sort exists here, it is unnecessary to inquire what excuse would be sufficient. The general rule, as above stated, seems on principle just. The person whose grass or corn is eaten down by the escaping cattle of his neighbour, or whose mine is flooded by the water from his neighbour's reservoir, or whose cellar is invaded by the filth of his neighbour's privy, or whose habitation is made unhealthy by the fumes and noisome vapours of his neighbour's alkali works, is damnified without any fault of his own; and it seems but reasonable and just that the neighbour who has brought something on his own property (which was not naturally there), harmless to others so long as it is confined to his own property, but which he knows will be mischievous if it gets on his neighbour's, should be obliged to make good the damage which ensues if he does not succeed in confining it to his own property. But for his act in bringing it there no mischief could have accrued, and it seems but just that he should at his peril keep it there, so that no mischief may accrue, or answer for the natural and anticipated consequence. And upon authority this we think is established to be the law, whether the things so brought be beasts, or water, or filth, or stenches."

My Lords, in that opinion, I must say I entirely concur. Therefore, I have to move your Lordships that the judgment of the Court of Exchequer Chamber be affirmed, and that the present appeal be dismissed with costs.

LORD CRANWORTH:

My Lords, I concur with my noble and learned friend in thinking that the rule of law was correctly stated by Mr. Justice *Blackburn* in delivering the opinion of the Exchequer Chamber. If a person brings, or accumulates, on his land anything which, if it should escape, may cause damage to his neighbour, he does so at his peril. If it does escape, and cause damage, he is responsible, however careful he may have been, and whatever precautions he may have taken to prevent the damage.

In considering whether a Defendant is liable to a Plaintiff for damage which the Plaintiff may have sustained, the question in general is not whether the Defendant has acted with due care and caution, but whether his acts have occasioned the damage. This is all well explained in the old case of **Lambert v. Bessey**, reported by Sir *Thomas Raymond* (Sir T. Raym. 421.). And the doctrine is founded on good sense. For when one person, in managing his own affairs, causes, however innocently, damage to another, it is obviously only just that he should be the party to suffer. He is bound. This is the principle of law applicable to cases like the present, and I do not discover in the authorities which were cited anything conflicting with it.

The doctrine appears to me to be well illustrated by the two modern cases in the Court of Common Pleas referred to by my noble and learned friend. I allude to the two cases of **Smith v. Kenrick (7 C. B. 564.)**, and **Baird v. Williamson (15 C. B. (N. S.) 376.)**. In the former the owner of a coal mine on the higher level worked out the whole of his coal, leaving no barrier between his mine and the mine on the lower level, so that the water percolating through the upper mine flowed into the lower mine, and obstructed the owner of it in getting his coal. It was held that the owner of the lower mine had no ground of complaint. The Defendant, the owner of the upper mine, had a right to remove all his coal. The damage sustained by the Plaintiff was occasioned by the natural flow or percolation of water from the upper strata. There was no obligation on the Defendant to protect the Plaintiff against this. It was his business to erect or leave a sufficient barrier to keep out the water, or to adopt proper means for so conducting the water as that it should not impede him in his workings. The water, in that case, was only left by the Defendant to flow in its natural course.

But in the later case of Baird v. Williamson the Defendant, the owner of the upper mine, did not merely suffer the water to flow through his mine without leaving a barrier between it and the mine below, but in order to work his own mine beneficially he pumped up quantities of water which passed into the Plaintiff's mine in addition to that which would have naturally reached it, and so occasioned him damage. Though this was done without negligence, and in the due working of his own mine, yet he was held to be responsible for the damage so occasioned. It was in consequence of his act, whether skilfully or unskillfully performed, that the Plaintiff had been damaged, and he was therefore held liable for the consequences. The damage in the former case may be treated as having arisen from the act of God; in the latter, from the act of the Defendant.

Applying the principle of these decisions to the case now before the House, I come without hesitation to the conclusion that the judgment of the Exchequer Chamber was right. The Plaintiff had a right to work his coal through the lands of Mr. Whitehead, and up to the old workings. If water naturally rising in the Defendants' land (we may treat the land as the land of the Defendants for the purpose of this case) had by percolation found its way down to the Plaintiff's mine through the old workings, and so had impeded his operations, that would not have afforded him any ground of complaint. Even if all the old workings had been made by the Plaintiff, he would have done no more than he was entitled to do; for, according to the principle acted on in **Smith v. Kenrick**, the person working the mine, under the close in which the reservoir was made, had a right to win and carry away all the coal without leaving any wall or barrier against *Whitehead's* land. But that is not the real state of the case. The Defendants, in order to effect an object of their own, brought on to their land, or on to land which for this purpose may be treated as being theirs, a large accumulated mass of water, and stored it up in a reservoir. The consequence of this was damage to the Plaintiff, and for that damage, however skilfully and carefully the accumulation was made, the Defendants, according to the principles and authorities to which I have adverted, were certainly responsible.

I concur, therefore, with my noble and learned friend in thinking that the judgment below must be affirmed, and that there must be judgment for the Defendant in Error.

Questions to be answered:

1. What are the facts of this case?
2. What is the issue of this case?
3. Describe the court's holding.
4. What is the reasoning of Lord Cranworth?
5. Describe the rule of law applied to resolve the issue.

Part II. Legal Translation (40 points)

Section A. Please translate the following Chinese into English.

（二）简化办案程序

近年来，诉讼案件大幅增加，人民法院在对案件性质、繁简程度综合考量的基础上，将案件进行繁简分流，不同案件适用不同的审理程序，使案件性质与审理程序相一致，促进了审判资源配置优化和诉讼效率提高。

扩大刑事案件简易程序的适用范围。2012年修改的刑事诉讼法将简易程序的适用范围，由可能判处三年有期徒刑以下刑罚的案件，扩大到基层人民法院管辖的刑事案件。

推进小额诉讼制度改革。为及时公正维护当事人合法权益，在部分基层人民法院开展小额速裁试点工作。试点法院在双方当事人自愿选择的前提下，对事实清楚、权利义务明确、争议标的金额较小的简单民事案件实行一审终审。在认真总结试点经验的基础上，2012年修改的民事诉讼法规定，基层人民法院审理的简单的民事案件，争议标的金额为各省、自治区、直辖市上年度就业人员年平均工资30%以下的民事案件，实行一审终审，从立法上肯定了小额诉讼的改革成果。

探索行政案件简易程序。人民法院对基本事实清楚、涉及财产金额较小、争议不大的一审行政案件，在双方当事人同意的前提下，可以实行独任审理，简化诉讼程序，立案之日起 45 日内结案。

（节选自《中国的司法改革》白皮书）

Section B. Please translate the following paragraphs into Chinese.

While the Hennepin County Attorney's Office assesses whether to charge Chinese billionaire Richard Liu with sexual assault, his alleged victim has told police he raped her in her apartment after a night of drinking as she pleaded with him to stop, the *Star Tribune* has learned.

News of Liu's arrest more than two months ago made headlines across the world and especially in China, where he is an internet entrepreneur and one of the country's wealthiest men. Few details of what happened that night have been made public, and Minneapolis police have declined to discuss the case. The County Attorney's Office has not set a timeline for when it will make a decision.

The *Star Tribune* has reviewed text messages, portions of the 21-year-old alleged victim's interviews with police, and other documents that piece together her account of the night leading up to Liu's arrest, which occurred when he was studying in an elite doctoral program for Chinese executives at the University of Minnesota's Carlson School of Management.

"I'm a normal student," the alleged victim begged Liu, according to an account she gave police regarding the Aug. 31 incident, shared by a source with the *Star Tribune*. "You have a family. I don't want to do that. I don't want to do this." "He didn't listen to me," she would go on to tell police.

Liu returned to China shortly after his release from jail. Jill Brisbois, a Minneapolis attorney who represents Liu, said that her client committed no wrongdoing.

The *Star Tribune* reviewed text messages the alleged victim sent from her apartment near campus.

"I didn't do it willingly ... I want to escape," she texted a friend in Mandarin, adding that Liu was in her bed. "I couldn't escape. How could I know that Qiangdong Liu would come to mess with me. I'm just a normal girl. I'm not eyeing anyone's deep pocket. I repeatedly begged him not to touch me."

Inside the apartment, she told police, he pulled off her sweater over her protests. She said that Liu told her she could be just like Wendi Deng, the Chinese-born ex-wife of Australian media executive Rupert Murdoch.

"I told him 'no' several times," she told police. She also told police that he tried to pull off her skirt and bra, held her arms and tried to throw her onto her bed.

"We were battling against each other on the bed and finally I escaped from him and went back to the living room and put the bra back on again," she said in the interview. "Finally, he just threw me onto the bed. He was on me. He was heavy. I tried to push him away. But he was on top of me … and then he raped me."

Darcy Horn, a spokeswoman for the Minneapolis Police, declined to comment, referring questions to the Hennepin County Attorney's Office.

"We've got the case," said Chuck , a spokesman for prosecutor's office. "We're looking it over closely. When we make a decision, we'll let everybody know."

Part III. Legal Writing (35 Points)

Suppose you are Jason Yang, a freshly admitted attorney in the State of California working for the law firm of Jepson, Hague, and Zhang in the city of Sacramento (which is located in California and in the Ninth Circuit). Your supervising partner, Dawn Guo, has asked you to conduct a preliminary review of the facts and applicable law in the case of Sherri Hezkeel, a model and former local television personality who lives in Los Angeles, California.

In 2004, Ms. Hezkeel first came to prominence when she won and subsequently co-hosted a locally televised (televised within the Greater Los Angeles area) game show called Epic. After subsequently co-hosting Epic for three years, Ms. Hezkeel turned to professional modeling, in which she has now dabbled for more than a decade. In 2016, Ms. Hezkeel had a relationship with an aspiring but relatively unknown rap musician, Skully Tack. Mr. Tack and Ms. Hezkeel dated for approximately nine months and were engaged to be married for two months before a very bitter breakup. However, they tried to keep their relationship while dating as well as their breakup as private as possible (initially). According to Ms. Hezkeel, Mr. Tack had a history of substance problems, most notably with alcohol. Although she claims he never physically assaulted her, he was, in her words, "extremely abusive verbally at times." Although the two crossed paths periodically for a while after their breakup, Ms. Hezkeel says she has not seen Mr. Tack in approximately two years.

During Ms. Hezkeel's modeling tenure, she has used her public platform to promote bullying awareness and anti-bullying initiatives. Last December, she was appointed as the head of California's anti-bullying commission. Three months before that appointment, Mr. Tack placed a post on Twitter, a popular social media platform, that read as follows:

"@sherrihezkeel is a phony. has no class. face is product of plastic surgery (i know). was a bully herself in high school. what a hypocrite."

The week following Ms. Hezkeel's appointment, Mr. Tack participated in a live television interview with a local Los Angeles television station. In the course of that interview, Mr. Tack was asked to clarify his social media post regarding Ms. Hezkeel's alleged bullying. However, he initially focused his comments on the first part of his post: "I mean, everyone can see [the effects of her] plastic surgery, right? Some of the surgeries have turned out real good, but the one she got a few years ago—she didn't say she had it, but I know she did—just look at the photos before and after and how obvious it is—it really distorted her cheekbones. She can't get the same modeling gigs anymore because of it, either. Again, I'm not really saying anything that isn't common knowledge to anyone with a pair of eyes and a little bit of common sense."

When pressed to rein his comments in and address the bullying issue, Mr. Tack said, "She told me once while we were engaged that in high school, she and her cheerleader friends used to make fun of the nerdy kids … I mean, really give them a hard time. They would put fake posters up featuring the 'weird' kids, especially the shy kids who hated talking in public, supporting them for student government. Then they'd taunt them about it. Stuff like, 'Oohh, hope you're ready for your big campaign speech next week. Everyone will be watching, you know.' Really cruel stuff like that. And even when she told me about it, it was like she was right back in that moment, still thought it was hilarious. So I think it's pretty ridiculous that she's now viewed as some anti-bullying saint."

Two days ago, an opinion column in a local newspaper was published with the headline, "Duplicity: Local Model Reportedly Finds Bullying a Joke, But Plastic Surgery Karma Puts the Joke on Her." The article contained several quotes from the televised interview with Mr. Tack.

Ms. Hezkeel has contacted Jepson, Hague, and Zhang to inquire about any potential recourse. According to her, it is true that she has had plastic surgery more than once, but she does not believe that this has had any negative impact on her appearance or ability to secure modeling assignments—at least prior to Mr. Tack's statements. She also claims that she never made any statements to Mr. Tack regarding past bullying, other than that she "may have told him that I was actually a victim of bullying during high school, which makes his false allegations hurt that much more."

Assume that in California, the elements of a defamation claim are: (1) publication of a statement of fact, (2) that is false, (3) unprivileged, (4) has a natural tendency to injure or which causes special damage, and (5) the defendant's fault in publishing the statement amounted to at least negligence.

Further assume that: (1) "public figures" are defined under California law as persons who have achieved such pervasive fame or notoriety to become a public figure for all purposes and in all contexts; and (2) "public officials" are defined under California law as persons who have or appear to have substantial responsibility for or control over the conduct of government affairs.

Further assume that whereas a private-figure plaintiff need show a minimum of negligence on the defendant's part, public officials and public figures need demonstrate actual malice.

Assume that the following abbreviated case opinions are also applicable:

Nizam-Aldine v. City of Oakland: With respect to defamation of a public figure, the plaintiff bears the burden of proving the falsity of the statement(s) at issue.

Smith v. Maldonado: In a case invoking matters of private concern only, the defendant bears the burden of proving the truth of the statement(s) at issue.

New York Times Co. v. Sullivan: Truth serves as an absolute defense against defamation.

Finally, assume that "substantial truth" is a defense recognized by California courts in defamation actions.

Please use these facts, the case authorities and legal precedents above, and your existing knowledge of U.S. law to draft an office memo to Dawn Guo, addressing the following.

1. What additional information is important to gather regarding the current fact pattern?
2. What, if any, additional information might you hope to uncover in a fuller reading of the above case opinions?
3. What, if any, additional legal issues should you research further?
4. Given the limited information above, what do you believe are the best potential paths of recourse for Ms. Hezkeel? What defenses might any defendant(s) raise, and how might Ms. Hezkeel's counsel respond to those possible defenses?

2018年11月法律英语证书（LEC）全国统一考试
参考答案

试 卷 一

1	C	21	C	41	C	61	A	81	B
2	D	22	C	42	C	62	B	82	A
3	A	23	B	43	A	63	D	83	D
4	B	24	B	44	C	64	C	84	B
5	B	25	C	45	C	65	D	85	C
6	D	26	D	46	C	66	C	86	C
7	B	27	C	47	D	67	D	87	C
8	B	28	B	48	D	68	A	88	C
9	A	29	D	49	C	69	B	89	C
10	A	30	D	50	D	70	A	90	C
11	B	31	C	51	A	71	C	91	B
12	A	32	C	52	D	72	A	92	B
13	B	33	B	53	B	73	A	93	C
14	D	34	B	54	C	74	A	94	D
15	D	35	D	55	C	75	B	95	B
16	D	36	C	56	D	76	D	96	D
17	C	37	A	57	A	77	A	97	A
18	B	38	A	58	D	78	C	98	C
19	C	39	B	59	C	79	D	99	A
20	B	40	A	60	A	80	A	100	A

附录一
2018年11月法律英语证书（LEC）全国统一考试试题及参考答案

试 卷 二

Part I. Case Reading and Comprehension
RULE OF LAW

A person who disrupts the natural state of real property by lawfully bringing something onto his land that, if it escapes, is capable of doing harm, is strictly liable for any harm occurring as a natural consequence of the escape.

FACTS

Fletcher (plaintiff) leased several underground coal mines from land adjacent to that owned by Rylands (defendant). Rylands owned a mill, and built a reservoir on his land for the purpose of supplying water to that mill. Rylands employed engineers and contractors to build the reservoir. In the course of building the reservoir, these employees learned that it was being built on top of abandoned underground coal mines. This fact was unknown by Rylands. After the reservoir was completed, it broke and flooded Fletcher's coal mines. This caused damage to Fletcher's property, and Fletcher brought suit against Rylands. Justices in the lower court differed as to whether Rylands should be liable, and the decision was appealed to the Court of Exchequer Chamber. There, Rylands was held strictly liable for damage caused to Fletcher's property by water from the broken reservoir. Rylands appealed.

ISSUE

Whether a person who disrupts the natural state of real property by lawfully bringing something onto his land that, if it escapes, can potentially do harm, is strictly liable for any harm caused by the escape.

HOLDING AND REASONING (Cairns, L.C.)

Yes. If Rylands' building of a reservoir on his property was an unnatural use of that property, Rylands is liable for damages caused to Fletcher's property. However, if, in the natural course of Rylands' use of his property, water accumulated either on the surface or underground and damages Fletcher's coal mine, Fletcher would not have an action for damages. The building of a reservoir to bring a large mass of water on Rylands' property may not be considered a natural use, as it impacts the amount of water that may potentially reach Fletcher's coal mine. Thus, Rylands may be liable for damages.

Part II. Legal Translation
Section A. Please translate the following Chinese into English.

Simplifying Case-Handling Procedures

Recent years have seen a sharp rise in litigation cases. On the basis of giving comprehensive consideration to the nature and complexity of the cases, the people's courts classified the cases into complex ones and simple ones and adopted different hearing procedures for different cases, thus applying different hearing procedures to cases of different natures to optimize judicial resources and enhance litigation efficiency.

Extending the scope of application of the summary procedures for criminal cases. The Criminal Procedure Law amended in 2012 extends the scope of application of the summary procedures from cases punishable by no more than three years in jail to all criminal cases under the jurisdiction of the local people's courts.

Promoting the reform of small-claim litigation. To safeguard the legitimate rights and interests of the parties concerned promptly and fairly, small-claim litigations are heard using simple procedures on a trial basis in some local people's courts. If both parties involved agree to use simple procedures, when the people's court hears a civil case in which the facts, rights and obligations are clear, and involves a small sum of money, the trial of first instance will be final. Based on previous experiences, the Civil Procedure Law amended in 2012 stipulates that among the simple civil cases heard by the local people's courts, if the sum of money involved is less than 30% of the annual average wage of employees in the previous year in the province (autonomous region or municipality directly under the central government) in question, then the trial of first instance will be final. This legislation affirms the reform of small-claim litigation.

Summary procedure for administrative cases. For an administrative case of first instance in which the basic facts are evident and the dispute is trivial in character, involving a small amount of property, the people's court may, on the premise of mutual agreement between the parties concerned, have a single judge try the case, simplify the litigation procedures, and conclude the case within 45 days after it is placed on the docket.

Section B. Please translate the following paragraphs into Chinese.

虽然亨内平县检察官办公室评估是否以性侵罪起诉中国亿万富翁刘强东，又名 Richard Liu，《星坛报》了解到：受害者已经告诉警察，那晚两人喝了很多酒，她恳求刘强东不要这样做，但他还是在她的公寓里强奸了她。

两个多月前刘被捕的消息成为世界各地的头条新闻，特别是在中国，他是一名互联网企业家，也是中国最富有的人之一。当晚发生的事情的细节很少公开，明尼阿波利斯警方拒绝讨论此案。县检察官办公室尚未确定何时做出决定。

《星坛报》查看了短信、21岁的受害者对警察的部分表述以及其他文件，这些文件将她在刘某被捕前的夜晚细节还原。当时刘正在明尼苏达大学卡尔森管理学院为中国高管举办的 DBA 课程中学习。

"我是一名普通学生，"根据她向警方提供的有关8月31日事件的描述，据称受害者向刘某请求，《星坛报》的一名消息人士也证实："你有家庭。我不想那样做。我不想这样做。""他根本不听我说，"她继续告诉警察。

刘从拘留所获释后不久回到了中国。代理刘案的明尼阿波利斯律师吉尔·布雷斯波丝说，她的客户没有犯下任何不法行为。

《星坛报》查看了据称受害人从校园附近的公寓发来的短信。

"我没有心甘情愿地去做……我想逃避，"她用中文给一位朋友发短信，并补充说刘在她的床上。"我无法逃脱。我怎么知道刘强东会侵扰我。我只是一个普通女孩。我不想要任何人的钱，我一再恳求他不要碰我。"

她告诉警方，在公寓内，刘在她的挣脱中脱下她的毛衣。她说，刘告诉她，她可以像中国出生的澳大利亚报业大亨鲁伯特·默多克的前妻邓文迪那样。

她告诉警方："我多次告诉他'不行'！"她还告诉警方，他试图脱下她的裙子和胸罩，抱着她的胳膊，试图将她扔到床上。

"我们在床上互相争斗，最后我逃离了他，然后跑到客厅，再次把胸罩穿上，"她在采访中说。"最后，他把我扔到了床上。他压在我身上，很沉重。我试图推开他。但他在我身上……然后他强奸了我。"

明尼阿波利斯警方发言人达西·霍恩拒绝置评，将问题提交给亨内平县检察官办公室。

"我们接到了这个案子，"检察官办公室发言人查克说。"我们正在密切关注它。当我们做出决定时，我们会公布于众。"

Part III. Legal Writing

请考生务必认真研读《法律英语写作教程》有关章节，注意写作格式和内容及字数要求。可参考教材附录的范文。

常用法律英语词汇及术语
GLOSSARY OF LEGAL TERMS

A

Absentia - Absent; proceeding without the defendant present.

Abstract of Title - A chronological summary of all official records and recorded documents affecting the title to a parcel of real property.

Abuse of Process - Tort no longer recognized in New Mexico. It has been combined with "Malicious Prosecution" to form a new tort, "Malicious Abuse of Process." See Malicious Abuse of Process.

Acceptance - An unambiguous communication that the offer has been accepted. For contracts controlled by the UCC, contracts involving the sales of goods need not mirror the offer's terms. For other contracts, the acceptance must mirror the offer's terms without omitting, adding, or altering terms. In other words, under the UCC, the acceptance may alter the terms of the offer without becoming a counteroffer.

Accomplice - (1) A partner in a crime. (2) A person who knowingly and voluntarily participates with another in a criminal activity.

Accord and Satisfaction - Compromise and settlement. A way to discharge a claim whereby the parties agree to give and accept something in settlement of the claim that will replace the terms of the parties' original agreement. Accord is the new agreement; satisfaction is performance of the new agreement.

Acknowledgment - (1) A statement of acceptance of responsibility. (2) The short declaration at the end of a legal paper showing that the paper was duly executed and acknowledged.

Acquit, Acquittal - A finding of not guilty by a judge or jury.

Action - Case, cause, suit, or controversy disputed or contested before a court.

Additur - An increase by a judge in the amount of damages awarded by a jury.

Adjudication - Judgment rendered by the court after a determination of the issues.

Ad Litem - A Latin term meaning "for the purpose of the lawsuit." For example, a guardian "ad litem" is a person appointed by the court to protect the interests of a minor or legally incompetent person in a lawsuit.

Administrator - (1) One who administers the estate of a person who dies without a will. (2) An official who manages a court.

Administrative Revocation - The taking of a driver's license by the Motor Vehicle Division, through law enforcement agents and administrative law judges without involvement by the courts.

Admissible Evidence - Evidence that can be legally and properly introduced in a civil or criminal trial.

Admonish - To advise or caution. For example the court may caution or admonish counsel or a witness for improper courtroom conduct.

Adversary System - The trial method used in the U.S. and some other countries. This system is based on the belief that truth can best be determined by giving opposing parties full opportunity to present and establish their evidence, and to test by cross-examination the evidence presented by their adversaries. This is done under the established rules of procedure before an impartial judge and/or jury.

Advisement - The process by which a judge takes time to consider, deliberate and/or consult on a matter prior to ruling.

Affiant - The person who makes and signs an affidavit.

Affidavit - A written statement of facts confirmed by the oath of the party making it, before a notary or officer having authority to administer oaths. For example, in criminal cases affidavits are often used by police officers asking courts to issue search or arrest warrants. In civil cases, affidavits of witnesses are often used to support motions for summary judgment.

Affidavit of Insolvency - A detailed form signed by the defendant, under oath, attesting to his/her indigency (inability to pay for private legal counsel).

Affirmative Defense - Apart from denying a charge or claim, a defendant may assert affirmative defenses such as insanity, self-defense or entrapment to avoid criminal responsibility, or assert the statute of limitations or bankruptcy to avoid civil liability.

Affirmed - A decision by an appellate court stating that the decision of the trial court is correct.

Aid and Abet - To actively, knowingly or intentionally assist another person in the commission or attempted commission of a crime.

Alford Plea - A plea to a criminal charge that does not admit guilt, but admits that sufficient evidence exists to obtain a conviction.

附录二
常用法律英语词汇及术语

Allegation - A statement of the issues in a written document (a pleading) that a person is prepared to prove in court. For example, an indictment contains allegations of crimes against the defendant.

Alleged - Stated; claimed; asserted; charged.

Alternative Dispute Resolution - Settling a dispute without a full or formal trial. Methods include mediation, conciliation, arbitration, and settlement facilitation, among others.

Amend - Improve, correct or change a complaint or other pleading.

Amicus Curiae - A friend of the court. One not a party to a case who volunteers, or is asked by the court, to offer information on a point of law or some other aspect of the case to assist the court in deciding a matter before it.

Answer - The defendant's response to the plaintiff's allegations as stated in a civil complaint. An item-by-item, paragraph-by-paragraph response to points made in a complaint; part of the pleadings.

Appeal - An application to a higher court for review of an order of conviction or of a civil judgment against a party.

Appeal Bond - A sum of money posted by a person appealing a judicial decision (appellant).

Appearance - (1) The formal proceeding by which a defendant submits to the jurisdiction of the court. (2) A written notification to the plaintiff by an attorney stating that s/he is representing the defendant.

Appellant - The party who takes an appeal from one court or jurisdiction to another.

Appellate Court - A court having jurisdiction to hear appeals and review a trial court's decision.

Appellee - The party against whom an appeal is taken. Sometimes called a respondent.

Arbitration - A form of alternative dispute resolution in which the parties bring their dispute to a neutral third party and agree to abide by his/her decision. In arbitration there is a hearing at which both parties have an opportunity to be heard.

Arraignment - Appearance of the defendant in criminal court to be advised of rights and enter a plea to the charges.

Arrest - The official taking of a person to answer criminal charges. This involves at least temporarily denying a person of liberty and may involve the use of force.

Arrest Warrant - An order by a judge that gives permission for a police officer to arrest a person for allegedly committing a crime.

Assault - Threat to inflict injury with an apparent ability to do so. Also, any intentional display of force that would give the victim reason to fear or expect immediate bodily harm.

Asylum State - The state holding a fugitive from justice in another state.

Attachment - Taking and holding a person's property during proceedings to ensure satisfaction of a judgment not yet rendered.

At Issue - Matters are "at issue" when the complaining party has stated his/her claim, the other side has responded with a denial, and the matter is ready to be tried.

Attempt - A person attempts to commit a crime when: (1) that person intended to commit the crime; and (2) began to do an act that constituted a substantial part of the crime, but failed to commit or complete the crime.

Attorney-at-Law - A licensed advocate or counsel authorized by the courts to prepare, manage and try cases in court, to prepare legal documents, or otherwise represent the interests of citizens.

Attorney-in-Fact - A private person (who is not necessarily a lawyer) authorized by another to act in his/her place, either for some particular purpose, as to do a specified act; or for the transaction of business in general, not of legal character. This authority is conferred by an instrument in writing, called a letter of attorney, or more commonly a power of attorney.

Attorney of Record - The attorney retained or assigned to represent a client.

B

Bail - Cash or surety posted to procure the release of a defendant in a criminal proceeding by insuring his/her future attendance in court, and compelling him/her to remain within the jurisdiction of the court.

Bail Bond - A document through which one agrees to accept responsibility for a defendant and insure his/her appearance in court. By signing the form, the person posting the bond agrees to forfeit the bond if the defendant fails to appear in court as ordered.

Bailiff - A court attendant who keeps order in the courtroom and has responsibility for the jury.

Bankruptcy - Refers to statutes and judicial proceedings involving persons or businesses that cannot pay their debts and seek the assistance of the court in getting a fresh start. Under the protection of the bankruptcy court, debtors may be released ("discharged") from their debts completely or allowed to repay them in whole or in part on a manageable schedule. Federal bankruptcy judges preside over these proceedings. The person with the debts is called the debtor and the people or companies to whom the debtor owes money are called creditors.

Bar - (1) Historically, the partition separating the general public from the space occupied by the judges, lawyers, and other participants in a trial. (2) More commonly, the body of lawyers within a jurisdiction.

Bar Examination - A state examination taken by prospective lawyers, qualifying them to be admitted to the bar and licensed to practice law.

Battery - A beating or other wrongful touching of a person. The threat to use force is an assault; actual use of force is a battery, which usually includes an assault.

Bench - The seat occupied by the judge; more broadly, the court or judicial branch itself.

Bench Trial - Trial without a jury in which a judge decides the facts as well as the law.

Bench Warrant - An order issued by a judge to arrest a person based on his/her failure to obey a court order. A bench warrant may be issued when a person fails to pay a fine, appear, or attend DWI School.

Beneficiary - Someone named to receive property or benefits in a will, trust, insurance policy, or other such document.

Bequeath - To give a gift to someone through a will.

Bequests - Gifts made in a will.

Best Evidence - Primary evidence; the best form of evidence available. Evidence short of this is "secondary." For example, the original of a letter is the "best evidence," while a photocopy is "secondary evidence."

Best Evidence Rule - Rule requiring parties to proffer the original writing, recording, or photograph when attempting to prove the contents thereof. However, a duplicate is admissible in place of an original unless there is a genuine question about the authenticity of the original or it would be unfair under the circumstances of the case to admit the duplicate instead of the original. Also, an original is not required if it is lost or destroyed, if it cannot be obtained through a subpoena, if it is in the possession of the opposing party, and if the original is not closely related to a controlling issue in the case.

Beyond a Reasonable Doubt - The standard in a criminal case requiring that the jury be satisfied to a moral certainty that every element of a crime has been proven by the prosecution. This standard of proof does not require that the state establish absolute certainty by eliminating all doubt, but it does require that the evidence be sufficiently conclusive that all reasonable doubts are removed from the mind or the ordinary person.

Bind over - To hold a person for trial on bond (bail) or in jail. If the judicial official conducting a preliminary hearing finds probable cause to believe the accused committed a crime, the official will bind over the accused, normally by setting bail for the accused's appearance at trial.

Bond (supersedeas) - The bond set by the court during the appeal procedure and posted with the Clerk of Court. It ensures payment to the winner at the trial court level if the appeal is unsuccessful.

Bond (surety) - A certificate posted by a bonding company to the law enforcement agency to secure the appearance in court of a criminal defendant.

Booking - The process of photographing, fingerprinting and recording identifying data of a suspect after arrest.

Breach - The breaking or violating of a law, right, or duty, either by the commission or omission of an act.

Breach of Contract - Failure by one party to abide by the terms of a contract without lawful excuse.

Brief - A written statement prepared by one side in a lawsuit to explain to the court its view of the facts of a case and the applicable law.

Burden of Proof - In the law of evidence, the necessity or duty of affirmatively proving a fact or facts in dispute on an issue raised between the parties in a lawsuit. The responsibility of proving a point or points: The level of the burden of proof for a type of case indicates the degree to which the point must be proven. For example, in a civil case the burden of proof rests with the plaintiff, who must establish his/her case by such standards of proof as a preponderance of evidence or clear and convincing evidence. In a criminal case, the burden on the prosecutor is to establish the defendant's guilty beyond a reasonable doubt, a much stricter standard.

C

Calendar - List of cases scheduled for hearing in court.

Calendaring - Assigning & scheduling of court appearances.

Capital Crime - A crime possibly punishable by death.

Caption - The heading on a legal document listing the parties, the court, the case number, and related information.

Case Law - Law established by previous decisions of appellate courts.

Cause - A lawsuit, litigation, or action. Any question, civil or criminal, litigated or contested before a court of justice.

Caveat - A warning; a note of caution.

Certified Copy - A copy of a document with a certificate attesting to its accuracy and completeness by the officer who has custody of the original.

Cert. Denied - Stands for "certiorari denied"; a writ of certiorari is a discretionary method by which a superior court chooses the cases it wishes to hear. "Cert. denied" means that the court has decided not to hear the case.

Certiorari - A means of getting an appellate court to review a lower court's decision when it is not required to do so. If an appellate court grants a writ of certiorari, it agrees to take the appeal. This is often referred to as "granting cert.," and results in an order to the lower court to convey the record of the case to the appellate court and to certify it as accurate and complete. Usually refers to a request for the Supreme Court to review a decision of the Court of Appeals.

Challenge - Term used in a jury trial for an attempt to exclude a potential juror.

Challenge for Cause - Objection to the seating of a particular juror for a stated reason (usually bias or prejudice for or against one of the parties in the lawsuit). The judge has the discretion to deny the challenge. Distinguished from peremptory challenge, which the party can usually exercise as a matter of right.

Chambers - A judge's private office. A hearing in chambers takes place in the judge's office outside of the presence of the jury and the public.

Change of Venue - Moving a lawsuit or criminal trial to another place for trial. Venue may be changed when a cases has received so much local publicity as to create a likelihood of bias in the jury pool.

Charge to the Jury - The judge's instructions to the jury explaining the law that applies to the facts of the case on trial.

Charges (multiple) - A case with more than one count or offense listed on the court file.

Charging Document - A citation, information, indictment or notice to appear, indicating that the named person committed a specific criminal offense or civil infraction.

Chief Judge - Presiding or administrative judge in a court.

Circumstantial Evidence - All evidence except eyewitness testimony. Evidence from which an inference must be drawn. Examples include documents, photographs, and physical evidence, such as fingerprints.

Citation - A written notice to appear in court, usually to answer a violation of traffic law or other minor criminal laws.

Civil Action - Non-criminal cases in which one private individual, business, or government sues another to protect, enforce, or redress private or civil rights.

Civil Contempt - Contempt can be civil or criminal depending on the purpose the court seeks to achieve through its punishment. Contempt is civil when the purpose of punishment is to coerce the defendant to perform an act previously ordered by the court, which the defendant has not done, such as paying child support. Compare with Criminal Contempt.

Civil Procedure - The set of rules and process by which a civil case is tried and appealed, including the preparations for trial, the rules of evidence and trial conduct, and the procedure for pursuing appeals.

Class Action - A lawsuit brought by one or more persons on behalf of a larger group.

Clear and Convincing Evidence - Standard of proof commonly used in civil lawsuits and in regulatory agency appeals. It governs the amount of proof that must be offered in order for the plaintiff to win the case. It imposes a greater burden than the preponderance of evidence standard, but less than the criminal standard "beyond a reasonable doubt."

Clemency or Executive Clemency - Act of grace or mercy by the president or governor to ease the consequences of a criminal act, accusation, or conviction. It may take the form of commutation or pardon.

Closing Argument - The closing statement, by counsel, to the trier of facts after all parties have concluded their presentation of evidence.

Codicil - An amendment to a will.

Collateral Estoppel - Rule that bars relitigation between the same parties of a particular issue or determinative fact when there is a prior judgment.

Commit - To send a person to prison, asylum, or reformatory by a court order.

Common Law - The legal system that originated in England and is now in use in the United States. It derives legal principles from the statements by judges in their written opinions, rather than from statutes enacted by legislative bodies.

Commutation - The reduction of a sentence, as from death to life imprisonment.

Co-Defendants - More than one person arrested and charged on the same criminal incident.

Comparative Negligence - A legal doctrine effective in New Mexico, by which acts of the opposing parties in a tort case are compared to determine the liability of each party, making each liable only for his/her percentage of fault. See also contributory negligence.

Compensatory Damages - Damages awarded to compensate the nonbreaching or injured party.

Competency to Stand Trial - In order to be competent to stand trial, a person must have the capacity to understand the nature and object of the proceedings, to consult with counsel, and to assist in preparing his/her defense. Due process prohibits the government from prosecuting a defendant who is not competent to stand trial.

Competent Witness - Every person is considered competent to be a witness. When a party questions the competency of a witness, the judge must determine the witness's capacity to observe, recall, and communicate what he or she witnessed, and that the witness understands the duty to be truthful.

Complainant - The party who complains or sues; one who applies to the court for legal redress. Also called the plaintiff.

Complaint - [Civil] The initial paperwork filed in a civil action that states the claim for which relief is sought; in the complaint the plaintiff states the wrongs allegedly committed by the defendant. [Criminal] A sworn written statement showing that the complaining person has reason to believe that the defendant has violated a criminal law.

Conciliation - A form of alternative dispute resolution in which the parties bring their dispute to a neutral third party, who helps lower tensions, improve communications, and explore possible solutions. Conciliation is similar to mediation, but it may be less formal.

Concurrent Jurisdiction - Authority vested in more than one court to hear and resolve specific types of disputes.

Concurrent Sentences - Sentences of imprisonment for conviction of more than one crime, to be served at the same time, rather than one after the other.

Condemnation - The legal process by which the government takes private land for a public use, paying the owners a fair price as determined by the court.

Conditions of Release - Conditions upon which an arrested person is released pending trial.

Consecutive Sentences - Successive sentences of imprisonment, one beginning at the expiration of another, imposed against a person convicted of two or more crimes.

Conservatorship - Legal right given to a person to manage the property and financial affairs of a person deemed incapable of doing that for himself/herself. (See also guardianship. Conservators have somewhat less responsibility than guardians.)

Consideration - A bargained-for benefit or right. Consideration may be a promise to perform a certain act—for example, a promise to deliver goods, a promise not to do something, payment, or a promise to pay money, among other things. Whatever its particulars, consideration must be something of value to the people who are making the contract.

Consolidation - Joinder of two or more separately filed criminal or civil complaints, so that the charges may be tried together.

Contempt of Court -Behavior intended to lessen the dignity of a court. Also, a willful act of disobedience of a judge's verbal or written order. There are two types of contempt, direct and indirect. When the contumacious (contemptuous) conduct occurs before the judge, the contempt is direct and may be punished summarily. All other conduct not witnessed by the judge is indirect contempt. Before punishing indirect contempt, the court must give the accused party notice and an opportunity to be heard. See also Civil Contempt and Criminal Contempt.

Continuance - Deferment of a trial or hearing to a later date.

Contraband - Articles, the possession of which is prohibited by law.

Contract - An agreement between two or more persons that creates an obligation to do or not to do a particular thing. A contract must have something of value promised or given, and a reasonable amount of agreement between the parties as to what the contract means. The parties must be legally capable of making binding agreements.

Contributory Negligence - A legal doctrine that prevents the plaintiff in a civil action from recovering against a defendant for his/her negligence if the plaintiff was also negligent. New Mexico has abandoned the doctrine of contributory negligence in favor of comparative negligence.

Conviction - A judgment of guilt against a criminal defendant.

Corpus Delicti - Body of the crime. The objective proof that a crime has been committed. It sometimes refers to the body of the victim of a homicide or to the charred shell of a burned house, but the term has a broader meaning. For the state to introduce a confession or to convict the accused, it must prove a corpus delicti, that is, the occurrence of a specific injury or loss and a criminal act as the source of that particular injury or loss.

Corroborating Evidence - Supplementary evidence that tends to strengthen or confirm the initial evidence.

Costs - Fees required in the course of a law suit, beginning with the docketing or filing fee, and may include service fees, witness fees, publication fees, etc. Does not include attorney fees.

Counsel - Legal adviser; a term used to refer to lawyers in a case.

Counterclaim - A claim made by the defendant in a civil lawsuit against the plaintiff. In essence, a counter lawsuit within a lawsuit.

Court - Government entity authorized to resolve legal disputes. Judges sometimes use "court" to refer to themselves in the third person, as in "the court has read the brief."

Court Administrator/Clerk of Court -An officer appointed by the court to oversee the administrative, non-judicial activities of the court.

Court Costs - The expenses of prosecuting or defending a lawsuit, other than the attorneys' fees. When permitted by law, a court may award an amount of money to the successful party, to be paid by the losing party, as reimbursement for the winner's court costs.

Court Recorder - A deputy clerk who maintains the verbatim record of court proceedings on tape.

Court Reporter - A certified person who maintains the verbatim record of court proceedings.

Court Rules - Procedural rules adopted by a court that govern the litigation process. Court rules often govern the format and style of documents submitted to the court.

Criminal Contempt - A criminal contempt is an act done in disrespect of the court or its process or which obstructs the administration of justice or tends to bring the court into disrepute. Criminal contempt can be direct or indirect. Direct contempt involves disorderly or insolent behavior in the presence of the judge that interferes with the course of a judicial proceeding; it is punishable summarily (i.e. without a hearing) by fine or imprisonment. Indirect contempt involves willful disobedience of court orders away from the court, which tend to impede justice. For example, refusing to carry out lawful court orders, preventing service of process, withholding evidence, and bribing a witness are all considered indirect criminal contempt. A person charged with indirect contempt is entitled to notice and a hearing.

Cross-Claim - A claim by codefendants or co-plaintiffs in a civil case against each other and not against persons on the opposite side of the lawsuit.

Cross-Examination - The questioning of a witness produced by the other side.

Cumulative Sentences - Sentences for two or more crimes to run consecutively, rather than concurrently.

Custody - Detaining of a person by lawful process or authority to assure his/her appearance at any hearing; the jailing or imprisonment of a person convicted of a crime.

D

Damages - Money awarded by a court to a person injured by the unlawful act or negligence of another person.

Decision - The judgment reached or given by a court of law.

Declaratory Judgment - A judgment of the court that explains what the existing law is or expresses the opinion of the court as to the rights and status of the parties, but which does not award relief or provide enforcement.

Decree - An order of the court. A final decree is one that fully and finally disposes of the litigation. An interlocutory decree is a preliminary order that often disposes of only part of a lawsuit.

Defamation - That which tends to injure a person's reputation. Libel is published defamation, whereas slander is spoken.

Default - A failure to respond to a lawsuit within the specified time.

Default Judgment - A judgment entered against a party who fails to appear in court or respond to the civil complaint or petition.

Defendant - In a civil case, the person being sued. In a criminal case, the person charged with a crime.

Deferred Sentence - A sentence that is postponed to a future time. After conviction, the judge does not announce or impose a sentence, but defers sentencing to a future date so that the defendant will complete certain conditions, such as attending driving school or completing a probationary period. If the person completes the requirements, the case will be dismissed and will not be part of the defendant's criminal record.

Deficiency Judgment - Judgment for a creditor for an amount equal to the difference between the amount owed by the debtor and the amount collected from sale of the collateral.

Demand for Discovery - Demand by the defense attorney to the prosecutor to furnish material information on a case.

Demanding State - The state seeking return of a fugitive.

De Novo - "Anew." A trial de novo is a new trial of a case, such as a district court trial de novo of a magistrate court case.

Deposition - An oral statement made before an officer authorized by law to administer oaths. Such statements are taken to examine potential witnesses, to obtain discovery to be used later in trial. Testimony of a witness other than in open court.

Descent and Distribution Statutes - State laws that provide for the distribution of estate property of a person who dies without a will. Same as intestacy laws.

Designee - A person appointed by a judge to act for the court to set conditions of release for any person arrested at a time when the judge is not available.

Direct Evidence - Proof of facts by witnesses who saw acts done or heard words spoken.

Direct Examination - The first questioning of witnesses by the party on whose behalf they are called.

Directed Verdict - Now called judgment as a matter of law. An instruction by the judge to the jury to return a specific verdict.

Disbarment - Form of discipline of a lawyer resulting in the loss (often permanently) of that lawyer's right to practice law. It is more severe than censure (an official reprimand or condemnation) and suspension (a temporary loss of the right to practice law.)

Discharge of bond - A court order to release a bond.

Disclaim - To refuse a gift made in a will.

Discovery - Investigation and gathering of information by opposing parties prior to going to trial. The tools of discovery include: interrogatories, depositions, production of documents or things, permission to enter land or other property, physical and mental examinations, and requests for admission.

Discretion - A power or right conferred on a judge to act according to the dictates of his own judgment and conscience, uncontrolled by the judgment or conscience of others.

Dismissal - An order or judgment disposing of a case without a trial.

- With prejudice - In criminal cases, the defendant may not be charged with the specific crime again. A case is usually dismissed with prejudice when the court has not pursued action within the six-month time limit. In civil cases, the complainant is barred from bringing the same claim or cause of action against the same defendant.
- Without prejudice - the person may be charged with the specific crime again. A case is usually dismissed without prejudice when more evidence is needed in a case or the case needs to be filed in another court because of jurisdictional issues. In civil cases, the plaintiff is entitled to bring the same claim or cause of action again.

Disposition - The sentencing or other final settlement of a case.

Dissent - (Verb) To disagree. (Noun) An appellate court opinion setting forth the minority view and outlining the disagreement of one or more judges with the decision of the majority.

Diversion - The process of removing some minor offenses from the full judicial process, on the condition that the accused undergo some sort of rehabilitation or make restitution for damages.

DOC - The Department of Corrections - state prison facility.

Docket - A list of cases to be heard by a court or a log containing brief entries of court proceedings.

Docket Call - The proceeding in which a judge assigns trial dates or takes pleas.

Docket Number - The numerical designation assigned to each case by the court.

Domicile - The place where a person has his/her permanent legal home. A person may have several residences, but only one domicile.

Double Jeopardy - Putting a person on trial more than once for the same crime. It is forbidden by the Fifth Amendment to the U.S. Constitution and by Article II, E of the NM Constitution.

Due Process of Law - The right of all persons to receive the guarantees and safeguards of the law and the judicial process. It includes such constitutional requirements as adequate notice of legal proceedings, opportunity to be heard by the judge, assistance of counsel, and the defendants' rights to remain silent, to a speedy and public trial, to an impartial jury and to confront and secure witnesses.

E

Elements of a Crime - Specific factors that define a crime and which the prosecution must prove beyond a reasonable doubt in order to obtain a conviction.

Eminent Domain - The power of the government to take private property for public use through condemnation.

En Banc - All the judges of a court sitting together. Appellate courts can consist of a dozen or more judges, but often they hear cases in panels of three judges. If a case is heard or reheard by the full court, it is heard en banc.

Endorsed - Stamped with the seal of the court indicating the date and time of filing with the court.

Enjoining - An order by the court telling a person to stop performing a specific act.

Entrapment - A defense to criminal charges alleging that agents of the government induced a person to commit a crime he/she otherwise would not have committed.

Entry of Judgment or Order - The filing of a written, dated and signed judgment or order.

Equal Protection of the Law - The guarantee in the Fourteenth Amendment to the U.S. Constitution Article III, and Article II, Section 18, of the NM Constitution, that the law treat all persons equally. Court decisions have established that this guarantee requires that courts be open to all persons on the same conditions, with like rules of evidence and modes of procedure; that persons be subject to no restrictions in the acquisition of property, the enjoyment of personal liberty, and the pursuit of happiness, which do not generally affect others; that persons are liable to no other or greater burdens than those are laid upon others; and that no different or greater punishment is enforced against them for a violation of the laws.

Equity - Generally, justice or fairness. Historically, equity refers to a separate body of law developed in England in reaction to the inability of the common-law courts, in their strict adherence to rigid writs and forms of action, to consider or provide a remedy for every injury. The king therefore established the court of chancery to do justice between parties in cases where the common law would give inadequate redress. The principle of this system of law is that equity will find a way to achieve a lawful result when legal procedure is inadequate. Remedies such as restraining orders and injunctions are equitable remedies. Equity and law courts are now merged in NM.

Escheat - The process by which a deceased person's property goes to the state if no heir can be found.

Escrow - Money or a written instrument such as a deed that, by agreement between two parties, is held by a neutral third party (held in escrow) until all conditions of the agreement are met.

Estate - An estate consists of personal property (car, household items, and other tangible items), real property and intangible property, such as stock certificates and bank accounts, owned in the individual name of a person at the time of the person's death. It does not include life insurance proceeds (unless the estate was made the beneficiary) or other assets that pass outside the estate (like a joint tenancy asset).

Estate Tax - Generally, a tax on the privilege of transferring property to others after a person's death. In addition to federal estate taxes, many states, including New Mexico, have their own estate taxes.

Estoppel - A person's own act, or acceptance of facts, which preclude his or her later making claims to the contrary.

Et al. - "And others."

Et Seq. - And the following.

Evidence - Testimony or exhibits received by the court at any stage of court proceedings.

Examination - The questioning of a witness under oath.

Exceptions - Declarations by either side in a civil or criminal case reserving the right to appeal a judge's ruling upon a motion or objection. These are no longer required to preserve error in New Mexico courts. Also, in regulatory cases, objections by either side to points made by the other side or to rulings by the agency or one of its hearing officers.

Exclusionary Rule - The rule preventing illegally obtained evidence, such as property found during an illegal search, from being used in any trial.

Execute - To complete the legal requirements (such as signing before witnesses) that make a will valid. Also, to execute a judgment or decree means to put the final judgment of the court into effect.

Executor - A personal representative, named in a will, who administers an estate.

Exempt Property - In collection, execution, and bankruptcy proceedings, this refers to certain property protected by law from the reach of creditors.

Exhibits - A document or item which is formally introduced in court and which, when accepted, is made part of the case file.

Exigent Circumstances - An emergency, demand, or need calling for immediate action or remedy that, for instance, would justify a warrantless search.

Exonerate - Removal of a charge, responsibility or duty.

Ex Parte - On behalf of only one party, without notice to any other party. For example, a request for a search warrant is an ex parte proceeding, since the person subject to the search is not notified of the proceeding and is not present at the hearing.

Ex Parte Communication - Communication about a lawsuit between a judge and one party, witness, attorney, or other person interested in the litigation when all of the parties are not present and the absent party did not have notice.

Ex Parte Proceeding - The legal procedure in which only one side is present or represented. It differs from the adversary system or adversary proceeding, and is only lawful in limited circumstances. For example, a hearing for a temporary restraining order.

Ex Post Facto - After the fact. The Constitution prohibits the enactment of ex post facto laws. These are laws that permit conviction and punishment for an act that was lawful at the time it was performed.

Express Warranty - An affirmation of fact or promise made by the seller to the buyer that is relied upon by the buyer in agreeing to the contract.

Expungement - Official and formal erasure of a record or partial contents of a record.

Extenuating Circumstances - Circumstances that render a crime less aggravated, heinous, or reprehensible than it would otherwise be.

Extradition - Surrender by one state to another of a person accused or convicted of an offense outside its own territory and within territorial jurisdiction of the other, with the other state which is competent to try him/her, demanding his/her surrender.

Extrinsic - Foreign, from outside sources.

F

Family Allowance - A small amount of money set aside from the estate of the deceased.

Its purpose is to provide for the surviving family members during the administration of the estate.

Felony - A crime that allows a defendant to be imprisoned for more than one year upon being found guilty.

Fiduciary - A person having a legal relationship of trust and confidence to another and having a duty to act primarily for the other's benefit: i.e., a guardian, trustee or executor.

File - To place a paper in the official custody of the clerk of court/court administrator to enter into the files or records of a case.

Filed in Open Court - Court documents entered into the file in court during legal proceedings.

Final Order - An order that ends the lawsuit between the parties, resolves the merits of the case, and leaves nothing to be done but enforcement.

Finding - Formal conclusion by a judge or regulatory agency on issues of fact. Also, a conclusion by a jury regarding a fact.

First Appearance - The initial appearance of an arrested person before a judge to determine whether or not there is probable cause for his/her arrest. Generally, the person comes before a judge within hours of the arrest. Also called initial appearance.

Foundation - Preliminary questions to a witness to establish admissibility of evidence; i.e., laying a foundation for admissibility.

Fraud - Intentional deception to deprive another person of property or to injure that person in some way.

Fruit of the Crime - Property acquired by means and in consequence of the commission of a crime, and sometimes constituting the subject matter of the crime.

Fruit of the Poisonous Tree - Property seized or statements made subsequent to and because of an illegal search or interrogation. Fruit of the poisonous tree is generally not admissible in evidence because it is tainted by the illegal search or interrogation.

Fugitive - A person who flees from one state to another to avoid prosecution.

G

Garnishment - A legal proceeding in which a debtor's money, which is in the possession of another (called the garnishee), is applied to the debts of the debtor, such as when an employer garnishes a debtor's wages.

General Damages - Compensation for the loss directly and necessarily incurred by a breach of contract.

General Jurisdiction - Refers to courts that have no limit on the types of criminal and civil cases they may hear.

Good Faith - Honest intent to act without taking an unfair advantage over another person. This term is applied to many kinds of transactions.

Good Time - A reduction in sentenced time in prison as a reward for good behavior. It usually is one-third to one-half off the maximum sentence.

Grand Jury - A jury of inquiry convened to determine whether evidence against a defendant justifies issuing an indictment; comprised of not more than 18 and not less than 15 persons, with at least 12 concurring before an indictment may be returned.

Grantor or Settlor - The person who sets up a trust. Also known as "trustor."

Guardian - A person appointed by will or by law to assume responsibility for incompetent adults or minor children. If one parent dies, the children's guardian will usually be the other parent. If both die, it usually will be a close relative.

Guardianship - Legal right given to a person to be responsible for the food, housing, health care, and other necessities of a person deemed incapable of providing these necessities for himself/herself. A guardian also may be given responsibility for the person's financial affairs, and thus perform additionally as a conservator. See also Conservatorship.

H

Habeas Corpus - A writ used as a means to bring a person before the court to determine whether he/she is being detained unlawfully.

Harmless Error - An error committed during a trial that was corrected or was not serious enough to affect the outcome of the trial and therefore was not sufficiently harmful (prejudicial) to require that the judgment be reversed on appeal.

Hearing - A proceeding, generally public, at which an issue of fact or law is discussed and either party has the right to be heard.

Hearsay - Testimony by a witness concerning events about which the witness has no personal knowledge. Hearsay testimony conveys not what the witness observed personally, but what others told the witness or what the witness heard others say. Hearsay is usually not admissible as evidence in court because of its unreliability.

Hung jury - Jury unable to reach a verdict. A trial ending in a hung jury results in a retrial with a new jury.

I

Immunity - A grant by the court assuring someone that they will not face prosecution in return for their providing criminal evidence.

Impeachment of a Witness - An attack on the credibility (believability) of a witness, through evidence introduced for that purpose.

Implied Consent - Knowing indirectly (through conduct or inaction) that a person would agree or give permission. For example, in New Mexico a person who gets a driver's license has given implied consent to allow a police officer to conduct an alcohol breath or blood test, when the police suspects the person is driving while intoxicated.

Implied Warranty of Merchantability - An assumption in law that the goods are fit for the ordinary purposes for which such goods are used. This implied warranty applies to every sale by a merchant who deals in goods of the kind sold. However, if there is a warning that the goods are sold "as is," the implied warranty does not apply.

Inadmissible - That which, under the rules of evidence, cannot be admitted or received as evidence.

In Camera - In chambers or in private. A hearing in camera takes place in the judge's office outside of the presence of the jury and the public.

Incarcerate - To confine in jail.

In-Custody Arraignments (jail cases) - Arraignment while the defendant remains in jail because defendant has not been released on bond or by other means.

Indeterminate Sentence - A sentence of imprisonment to a specified minimum and maximum period of time, specifically authorized by statute, subject to termination by a parole board or other authorized agency after the prisoner has served the minimum term.

Indicia - Signs, indications.

Indictment - The written accusation by a grand jury that charges a person named in the indictment with the violation of a law. Indictments are used for felony charges, not misdemeanors.

Indigency - Financial inability to hire a lawyer or pay court costs.

Indigent - Needy or impoverished. A defendant who can demonstrate his/her indigence to the court may be assigned a court-appointed attorney at public expense in criminal and child abuse/neglect cases, but not in other civil cases.

In Forma Pauperis - "In the manner of a pauper." Permission given to a person to sue without payment of court costs because of indigence or poverty.

Information - An accusation against a person for a criminal offense, without an indictment; presented by the prosecution instead of a grand jury. Informations are used for felony charges, not misdemeanors.

Infra - Below.

Infraction - A violation of law not punishable by imprisonment. Minor traffic offenses generally are considered infractions.

Inheritance Tax - A state tax on property that an heir or beneficiary under a will receives from a deceased person's estate. The heir or beneficiary pays this tax.

Initial Appearance - In criminal law, the hearing at which a judge determines whether there is sufficient evidence against a person charged with a crime to hold him/her for trial. The Constitution bans secret accusations, so initial appearances are public unless the defendant asks otherwise; the accused must be present, though he/she usually does not offer evidence. Also called first appearance.

Injunction - Writ or order by a court prohibiting a specific action from being carried out by a person or group. A preliminary injunction is granted provisionally, until a full hearing can be held to determine if it should be made permanent.

Inspectorial Search - An entry into and examination of premises or vehicles by an inspector for the identification and correction of conditions dangerous to health or safety.

Instructions - Judge's explanation to the jury before it begins deliberations of the questions it must answer and the applicable law governing the case. Also called charge to the jury.

Intangible assets - Nonphysical items that have value, such as stock certificates, bonds, bank accounts, and pension benefits. Intangible assets must be taken into account in estate planning and divorce.

Interlocutory - Provisional; not final. An interlocutory order or an interlocutory appeal concerns only a part of the issues raised in a lawsuit.

Interpleader - An action in which a third person asks the Court to determine the rights of others to property held—but not owned—by the third person.

Interrogatories - Written questions asked by one party in a lawsuit for which the opposing party must provide written answers.

Intervention - An action by which a third person that may be affected by a lawsuit is permitted to become a party to the suit.

Inter Vivos Gift - A gift made during the giver's life.

Inter Vivos Trust - Another name for living trust.

Intestacy Laws - See Descent and Distribution Statutes.

Intestate - Dying without having a will.

Intestate Succession - The process by which the property of a person who has died without a will passes on to others according to the state's descent and distribution statutes. If someone dies without a will and the court uses the state's intestate succession laws, an heir who receives some of the deceased's property is an intestate heir.

Invoke the Rule   - Separation and exclusion of witnesses (other than parties) from the courtroom.

Irrevocable Trust   - A trust that, once set up, the grantor may not revoke.

Issue   - (1) The disputed point in a disagreement between parties in a lawsuit. (2) To send out officially, as in to issue an order.

J

Joinder   - Combining charges or defendants on the same complaint. Where a crime is committed by two people, both may be charged on one complaint. Joinder also applies in civil cases, where parties and claims may be joined in one complaint.

Joint and Several Liability   - A legal doctrine that makes each of the parties who are responsible for an injury liable for all the damages awarded in a lawsuit if the other responsible parties cannot pay.

Joint Tenancy   - A form of legal co-ownership of property (also known as survivorship). At the death of one co-owner, the surviving co-owner becomes sole owner of the property. Tenancy by the entirety is a special form of joint tenancy between a husband and wife.

Judge   - An elected or appointed public official with authority to hear and decide cases in a court of law. A judge Pro Tem is a temporary judge.

Judgment   - The first disposition of a lawsuit.

- **Consent Judgment**   - Occurs when the provisions and terms of the judgment are agreed on by the parties and submitted to the court for its sanction and approval.
- **Default Judgment**   - A judgment rendered because of the defendant's failure to answer or appear.
- **Judgment Notwithstanding the Verdict**   - Judgment entered by order of the court for one party notwithstanding the jury's verdict in favor of the other party. A judgment notwithstanding the verdict may only arise after a motion for a directed verdict.
- **Judgment on the Pleadings**   - Judgment based on the pleadings alone. It is used when there is no dispute as to the facts of the case and one party is entitled to a judgment as a matter of law.
- **Summary Judgment**   - Judgment given on the basis of pleadings, affidavits, and exhibits presented for the record without any need for a trial. As with Judgment on the Pleadings, it is used when there is no dispute as to the facts of the case and one party is entitled to a judgment as a matter of law.

- Judgment and Sentence - The official document of a judge's disposition of a case sentencing a defendant to the Department of Corrections or jail custody.

Judicial Review - The authority of a court to review the official actions of other branches of government. Also, the authority to declare unconstitutional the actions of other branches.

Jurat - Certificate of officer or person whom writing was sworn before. Typically, "jurat" is used to mean the certificate of the competent administering officer that writing was sworn to by person who signed it.

Jurisdiction - The court's legal authority to hear and resolve specific disputes. Jurisdiction is usually composed of personal jurisdiction (authority over persons) and subject matter jurisdiction (authority over types of cases.)

Jurisprudence - The study of law and the structure of the legal system.

Juror Disqualified - Juror excused from a trial.

Jury - Persons selected according to law and sworn to inquire into and declare a verdict on matters of fact. A petit jury is a trial jury, composed of 6 to 12 persons, which hears either civil or criminal cases.

Jury Array - The whole body of prospective jurors summoned to court from which the jury will be selected. Also called "Jury Panel."

Jury List - A list containing the names of jurors empanelled to try a cause or containing the names of all the jurors summoned to attend court.

Jury Polling - The procedure by which each individual juror is asked to affirm his or her verdict in open court at the conclusion of a trial.

Jury Trial - A trial in which the jury judges the facts and the judge rules on the law.

Justiciable - Issues and claims capable of being properly examined in court.

Juvenile - A person under 18 years of age.

K

Kangaroo Court - Term descriptive of a sham legal proceeding in which a person's rights are totally disregarded and in which the result is a foregone conclusion because of the bias of the court or other tribunal.

Knowingly and Willfully - This phrase, in reference to violation of a statute, means consciously and intentionally.

L

Lapsed Gift - A gift made in a will to a person who has died prior to the will-maker's death.

Larceny - Obtaining property by fraud or deceit.

附录二
常用法律英语词汇及术语

Law - The enforceable rules that govern individual and group conduct in a society. The law establishes standards of conduct, the procedures governing standards of conduct, and the remedies available when the standards are not adhered to.

Law Clerks - Persons trained in the law who assist judges in researching legal opinions.

Leading Question - A question that suggests the answer desired of the witness. A party generally may not ask one's own witness leading questions. Leading questions may be asked only of adverse witnesses and on cross-examination.

Legal Aid - Professional legal services available usually to persons or organizations unable to afford such services.

Leniency - Recommendation for a sentence less than the maximum allowed.

Lesser Included Offense - Any lesser offense included within the statute defining the original charge, such as a lower grade of an offense. An offense composed of some, but not all of the elements of a greater offense and which does not have any additional elements not included in the greater offense, so that it is impossible to commit the greater offense without also committing the lesser.

Letters of Administration - Legal document issued by a court that shows an administrator's legal right to take control of assets in the deceased person's name. Used when the deceased died without a will.

Letters Testamentary - Legal document issued by a court that shows an executor's legal right to take control of assets in the deceased person's name. Used when the deceased left a will.

Liable - Legally responsible.

Libel - Published words or pictures that falsely and maliciously defame a person. Libel is published defamation; slander is spoken.

Lien - A legal claim against another person's property as security for a debt. A lien does not convey ownership of the property, but gives the lien-holder a right to have his or her debt satisfied out of the proceeds of the property if the debt is not otherwise paid.

Limited Jurisdiction - Courts with limited jurisdiction may hear only certain kinds of cases and are precluded from hearing anything else. For example, small claims court may only decide cases in which the amount in controversy is below a set figure.

Lis Pendens - A pending suit. Jurisdiction, power, or control that courts acquire over property in a suit pending action and until final judgment.

Litigant - A party to a lawsuit. Litigation refers to a case, controversy, or lawsuit.

Living Trust - A trust set up and in effect during the lifetime of the grantor. Also called inter vivos trust.

M

Magistrate - A judge whose civil and criminal jurisdiction is limited by law. In federal court, a judicial officer who is assigned numerous trial and pretrial responsibilities.

Malfeasance - Evil doing, ill conduct; the commission of some act which is positively prohibited by law.

Malicious Abuse of Process - Tort involving a litigant's malicious misuse of the power of the judiciary. The elements of this tort are: (1) initiation of judicial proceedings against the plaintiff by the defendant; (2) an act by the defendant in the use of process that would not be proper in the regular prosecution of the claim; (3) a primary motive by the defendant in misusing the process to achieve an illegitimate end; and (4) damages.

Malicious Prosecution - In New Mexico, the tort of "Malicious Prosecution" no longer exists. It has been combined with "Abuse of Process" to form a new tort, "Malicious Abuse of Process." See Malicious Abuse of Process.

Mandamus - A writ issued by a court ordering a public official to perform an act that s/he is required to do by law under the existing state of facts.

Mandate - The official decree by a court of appeal.

Manslaughter - The unlawful killing of another without intent to kill; either voluntary (upon a sudden impulse); or involuntary (during the commission of an unlawful act not ordinarily expected to result in great bodily harm.)

Mediation - A form of alternative dispute resolution in which the parties bring their dispute to a neutral third party, who helps them reach a resolution.

Memorialized - In writing.

Mens Rea - The "guilty mind" necessary to establish criminal responsibility.

Merchant - A person who regularly deals in goods of the kind being sold or who otherwise holds himself out as having a special knowledge of the goods sold. For example, Bob owns a clock shop and sells clocks, so he would be considered a merchant of clocks. However, if Bob sold his car to someone, he would not be considered a merchant of cars.

Merger Clause - Merger clauses state that the written document contains the entire understanding of the parties. The purpose of merger clauses is to ensure that evidence outside the written document will not be admissible in court to contradict or supplement the express terms of the written agreement.

Merits - The substantive claims and defenses raised by the parties to an action.

Minor - A person under 18 years of age.

Miranda Warning - Prior to any custodial interrogation (that is, questioning by police after a person has been deprived of his or her freedom in a significant way), a person must be advised that: (1) he has a right to remain silent; (2) any statement he does make may be used in evidence against him; (3) he has the right to the presence of an attorney; and (4) if cannot afford an attorney, one will be appointed for him prior to any questioning, if he so desires.

Misdemeanor - An offense punishable by not more than one year in county jail and/or $1,000 fine.

Mistrial - An invalid trial, caused by fundamental error or inability of a jury to reach a verdict. When a mistrial is declared, the trial must start again from the selection of the jury.

Mitigating Circumstances - Those facts which do not constitute a justification or excuse for an offense but which may be considered as reasons for reducing the degree of blame.

Mitigation - Reduction of penalty or punishment.

Moot - A moot case or a moot point is one not subject to a judicial determination because it involves an abstract question, because there is no actual controversy, or because the issues no longer exist. Mootness usually refers to a court's refusal to consider a case because the issue involved has been resolved prior to the court's decision, leaving nothing that would be affected by the court's decision.

Motion - Oral or written request made by a party to an action before, during, or after a trial, upon which a court issues a ruling or order.

Motion in Limine - A motion made outside the presence of a jury requesting that the court not allow certain evidence that might prejudice the jury. Usually heard before trial begins.

Motion to Expunge - A motion to delete material from official court records, such as a record of juvenile conviction.

Motion to Mitigate Sentence - A motion to reduce the sentence.

Motion to Seal - A motion to close records to public inspection.

Motion to Suppress - A motion to prevent admission of evidence in a case.

Murder - The unlawful killing of a human being with deliberate intent to kill. Murder in the first degree is characterized by premeditation; murder in the second degree is characterized by a sudden and instantaneous intent to kill or to cause injury without caring whether the injury kills or not.

Mutuality - A meeting of the minds of contracting parties regarding the material terms of the agreement.

N

Necessarily Included Offense - Where an offense cannot be committed without necessarily committing another offense, the latter is a necessarily included offense; sometimes referred to as lesser included offense.

Negligence - Failure to exercise the degree of care that a reasonable person would exercise under the same circumstances.

Next Friend - One acting without formal appointment as guardian for the benefit of an infant, a person of unsound mind not judicially declared incompetent, or other person under some disability.

No-Contest Clause - Language in a will providing that a person who makes a legal challenge to the will's validity will be disinherited.

No Contest Plea - See Nolo Contendere.

No-Fault Proceedings - A civil case in which parties may resolve their dispute without a formal finding of error or fault.

Nolle Prosequi - The prosecutor declines to prosecute, but may still initiate prosecution within the time allowed by law.

Nolo Contendere - No contest. A plea through which the defendant does not admit guilt, but which has the same legal effect as a plea of guilty in a criminal case. However, the no contest plea may not be used in a civil action related to the criminal charge to prove the defendant's civil liability. For example, a plea of nolo contendere for a traffic citation that resulted from an accident cannot be used to convince a judge in a civil case that the defendant is guilty of causing an accident.

Non-jury trial - A case tried by a judge on the facts as well as the law.

No Probable Cause - Insufficient grounds to hold the person who was arrested.

Notice - Formal notification to the party that has been sued that a civil lawsuit has been filed. Also, any form of notification of a legal proceeding or filing of a document.

Notice of Lis Pendens - A notice filed on public records to warn all persons that the title to certain property is in litigation, and that if they purchase or lease that property they are in danger of being bound by an adverse judgment. The notice is for the purpose of preserving rights pending litigation.

Nuisance - An unreasonable, unwarranted, or unlawful use of one's property that annoys, disturbs, or inconveniences another in the use of his or her property. Violation of an ordinance that forbids annoyance of the public in general.

Nunc Pro Tunc - An entry made now for an act done previously and to have the effect as if it were done on a prior date.

Nuncupative Will - An oral (unwritten) will.

O

Oaths - Sworn attestations required in court, usually administered by the in-court clerk.

Objection - The process by which one party tries to prevent the introduction of evidence or the use of a procedure at a hearing. An objection is either sustained (allowed) or overruled by the judge.

Offense - A violation of a municipal ordinance or state statute.

Offer - An expression of willingness to enter into a bargain that is definite and certain in its terms and that is communicated to the offeree. Once accepted, the offer is transformed into a contractual obligation.

Offeree - The person to whom an offer is made.

Offeror - The person who makes an offer.

Opening Statement - The initial statement made by attorneys for each side, outlining the facts each intends to establish during the trial.

Opinion - A judge's written explanation of a decision of the court or of a majority of judges. A dissenting opinion disagrees with the majority opinion because of the reasoning and/or the principles of law on which the decision is based. A concurring opinion agrees with the decision of the court but offers further comment or different reasoning. A per curiam opinion is an unsigned opinion "of the court."

Oral Argument - An opportunity for lawyers to summarize their positions before the court and also to answer the judges' questions.

Order - A written or oral command from a court directing or forbidding an action.

Ordinance - A law adopted by the governing body of a municipality or county.

Overrule - A judge's decision not to allow an objection. Also, a decision by a higher court finding that a lower court decision was in error.

P

Parens Patriae - The doctrine under which the court protects the interests of a juvenile.

Parol Evidence - Oral evidence.

Parol Evidence Rule - When a written agreement is intended to be a complete and final document, then the terms of the agreement cannot be altered by evidence of oral (parol) agreements that purport to change, explain, or contradict the written agreement.

Parole - The supervised conditional release of a prisoner before the expiration of his/her sentence. If the parolee observes the conditions, he/she need not serve the rest of his/her term.

Party - A person, business, organization or government agency involved in the prosecution or defense of a legal proceeding.

Patent - A government grant giving an inventor the exclusive right to make or sell his/her invention for a term of years.

Penalty Assessment - Procedure in which traffic offender is allowed to mail in a fine (plead guilty by mail). Points may be assessed against the person's driving record for penalty assessment offenses.

Peremptory Challenge - The right to challenge a judge or prospective juror without assigning a reason for the challenge.

Perjury - The criminal offense of making a false statement under oath.

Permanent Injunction - A court order requiring that some action be taken or that some party refrain from taking action for an indefinite period.

Personal Jurisdiction - Power which a court has over the defendant's person and which a court must have before it can enter a judgment affecting the defendant's rights.

Per Se Law - In the Motor Vehicle Code, the per se crime is driving with a blood alcohol level of .08 or greater, as established through a valid testing procedure. No proof is required to show that the defendant was under the influence since the law concludes that driving with a blood alcohol content (BAC) of .08 or greater is driving while intoxicated. (DWI can be proved by other evidence even if a defendant's BAC is less than .08.)

Personal Property - Tangible physical property (such as cars, clothing, furniture and jewelry) and intangible personal property (such as bank accounts). This does not include real property such as land or rights in land.

Personal Recognizance - In criminal proceedings, the pretrial release of a defendant without bail upon his/her promise to return to court. See also Release on Own Recognizance.

Personal Representative - The person that administers an estate. If named in a will, that person's title is an executor. If there is no valid will, that person's title is an administrator.

Petitioner - The person filing an action in a court of original jurisdiction. Also, the person who appeals the judgment of a lower court. The opposing party is called the respondent.

Petty Misdemeanor - A crime that allows less than six months of jail time upon conviction.

Plaintiff - The person/business/organization/agency that files the complaint in a civil lawsuit. Also called the complainant.

Plain View Doctrine - The doctrine that permits a law enforcement officer to lawfully seize incriminating evidence not specifically sought but readily visible in the course of a valid search.

Plea - (1) Defendant's answer to the charge—guilty, not guilty, nolo contendere or Alford plea. (2) In a criminal proceeding, the defendant's declaration in open court that he or she is guilty or not guilty. The defendant's answer to the charges made in the indictment or information.

Plea Agreement - An agreement between the prosecutor and the defendant, presented for the court's approval, regarding the sentence the defendant should serve upon a plea of guilty, an Alford plea, or a no contest plea. Typically, the defendant pleads guilty in exchange for some form of leniency. For example, the defendant may plead to lesser charges so that the penalties are diminished. Or, the defendant may plead to some, but not all of the charges so that others are dropped. The agreement may include sentencing recommendations. Such bargains are not binding on the court.

Plea Bargaining or Plea Negotiating - The process through which an accused person and a prosecutor negotiate a mutually satisfactory disposition of a case. The Court is not privy to the actual negotiations, but is presented with a plea agreement for its approval or rejection.

Pleadings - The written statements of fact and law filed by the parties to a lawsuit.

Points or Point Information - Penalty points imposed by the Motor Vehicles Division after conviction of a traffic offense.

Polling the Jury - The act, after a jury verdict has been announced, of asking jurors individually whether they agree with the verdict.

Pour-Over Will - A will that leaves some or all estate assets to a trust established before the will-maker's death.

Prejudice - Unfair harm to one party.

Power of Attorney - Formal authorization of a person to act in the interests of another who is incapable of managing his or her own affairs or property.

Preliminary Hearing - See "Initial Appearance."

Preliminary Injunction - Court order requiring action or forbidding action until a decision can be made whether to issue a permanent injunction. It differs from a temporary restraining order.

Pre-Sentence Investigation - A background investigation of the defendant by the Department of Corrections, returnable to the sentencing judge on or before a certain date.

Pre-Sentence Report - A report designed to assist the judge in passing sentence on a convicted defendant. Such reports should contain at least the following: (1) complete description of the situation surrounding the criminal activity; (2) offender's educational background; (3) offender's employment background; (4) offender's social history; (5) residence history of the offender; (6) offender's medical history; (7) information about environment to which the offender will return; (8) information about any resources available to assist the offender; (9) probation officer's view of the offender's motivations and ambitions; (10) full description of the offender's criminal record; and (11) recommendation as to disposition.

Pretermitted Child - A child born after a will is executed, who is not provided for by the will. New Mexico law provides for a share of estate property to go to such children.

Pretrial Conference - A meeting between the judge and the lawyers involved in a lawsuit to narrow the issues in the suit, agree on what will be presented at the trial, and explore the possibility of settling the case without a trial.

Pretrial Intervention - Programs to aid certain qualifying criminal defendants by diverting them from prosecution and enrolling them in rehabilitative programs. Upon successful completion of the required program(s), the criminal case is dismissed. Pretrial intervention is most often used in substance abuse and domestic violence where the crime charged is the defendant's first offense.

Pretrial Release - Release by sheriff's personnel after arrest and before any court appearance, but with a court appearance date.

Precedent - A previously decided case that guides the decision of future cases; source of common law.

Preponderance of the evidence - Evidence that is of greater weight or more convincing than the evidence that is offered in opposition to it. The amount of evidence that must be presented to prevail in most civil actions.

Presentment - Declaration or document issued by a grand jury that either makes a neutral report or notes misdeeds by officials charged with specified public duties. It ordinarily does not include formal criminal charges.

Prima Facie - Presumably. A fact presumed to be true unless disproved by some evidence to the contrary. Evidence that will prevail until contradicted and overcome by other evidence. A prima facie case is one in which the plaintiff has presented sufficient evidence to require the defendant to go forward with his or her case. In other words, the plaintiff will prevail if the defendant does not rebut the plaintiff's case.

Principal - The person primarily liable; the person for whom performance of an obligation a surety has become bound.

Privilege - A right, power, or immunity held by a person or class beyond the course of law, such as the privilege against self-incrimination under the Fifth Amendment.

Probable Cause - The evidence required before a person or property may be searched or seized by law enforcement and before a search or arrest warrant may be issued.

- Probable Cause to Arrest exists when the facts and circumstances within the officers' knowledge and of which the officers had reasonably trustworthy information are sufficient to warrant a person of reasonable caution to believe that the suspect has committed or is committing a crime.

- Probable Cause to search exists when the facts and circumstances within the officers' knowledge and of which the officers had reasonably trustworthy information are sufficient to warrant a person of reasonable caution to believe that evidence of a crime will be found in the location identified.

Probate - The court-supervised process by which a will is determined to be the will-maker's final statement regarding how the will maker wants his/her property distributed. It also confirms the appointment of the personal representative of the estate. Probate also means the process by which assets are gathered; applied to pay debts, taxes, and the expenses of administration; and distributed to those designated as beneficiaries in the will.

Probate Court - The court with jurisdiction to supervise estate administration.

Probate Estate - Estate property that may be disposed of by a will.

Probation - A procedure under which a defendant convicted of a crime is released by the court without imprisonment under a suspended or deferred sentence and subject to conditions.

Probative Value - Evidence has probative value if it tends to prove an issue. It is evidence that furnishes, establishes, or contributes toward proof.

Pro Bono Publico - For the public good. Lawyers representing clients without a fee are said to be working pro bono publico.

Promissory Estoppel - Equitable doctrine allowing the court to enforce a promise even though a valid contract was not formed when a person reasonably acted in reliance on that promise. Promissory Estoppel allows the court to compensate the person for their expenditures and/or to avoid the unjust enrichment of the other party.

Property Bond - A signature bond secured by mortgage or real property.

Pro Se - On one's own behalf, commonly used to refer to a party representing himself or herself in a court action, instead of being represented by an attorney.

Prosecutor - A trial lawyer representing the government in a criminal case and the interests of the state in civil matters. In criminal cases, the prosecutor has the responsibility of deciding who and when to prosecute.

Proximate Cause - The act that caused an event to occur. A person generally is liable only if an injury was proximately caused by his/her action or by his/her failure to act when he/she had a duty to act.

Public Defender - A court-appointed attorney for those defendants who are declared indigent.

Punitive Damages - Damages awarded over and above compensatory damages in order to punish the defendant for malicious, wanton, willful, reckless, oppressive, or fraudulent conduct. Punitive damages are imposed to compensate the Plaintiff for mental anguish, shame, degradation, or other aggravations beyond actual damages.

Q

Qualified disclaimer - An irrevocable and absolute refusal to accept a particular interest in the estate of a decedent (as a spouse) that is made in accordance with federal tax requirements and results in favorable tax consequences (as exemption from a gift tax)

Qualifying date - The date which the Visa Office of the Department of State uses the qualifying date to determine when to send the Instruction Package to an immigrant visa applicant. The Instruction Package tells the applicant what documents need to be prepared for the immigrant visa application.

Qualifying event - An event or condition (as a terminal illness) that permits an acceleration or continuation of benefits or coverage, *esp.* an event involving an employee covered by a group health insurance plan that would result in a termination of coverage for the employee or a qualified beneficiary if not for federal provisions for the continuation of such coverage (as for six months).

Qualifying widow(er) - The filing status used by a qualified person for the two years following a spouse's death.

Quash - To vacate or void a summons, subpoena, etc.

Queen's bench - A division of the High Court of Justice of England and Wales that hears civil cases (as commercial cases) and appeals of criminal cases used during the reign of a queen compare king's bench

Qui tam action - An action that is brought by a person on behalf of a government against a party alleged to have violated a statute esp. against defrauding the government through false claims and that provides for part of a penalty to go to the person bringing the action [the whistleblower brought a *qui tam action* against the contractor for presenting fraudulent claims for payment]

Quittance - Exoneration; a release.

Quorum - A majority; the number of people who must be present to permit an organization, a group, a body, etcetera, to conduct its business and reach valid decisions.

Quota - (1) The proportional part of a whole that is owned to a person, or to a group of people or to a particular district or state. (2) The limited number of people that are permitted to emigrate to this country from various foreign countries. Each country has its own number, or quota, allotted to it.

R

Real Property - Land, buildings, and other improvements affixed to the land.

Reasonable Belief - Probable cause. The facts and circumstances within an arresting officer's knowledge, and of which s/he had reasonably trustworthy information, sufficient in themselves to justify a person of average caution in believing that a crime has been or is being committed. Facts sufficient to justify a warrantless arrest.

Reasonable Doubt - Such a doubt as would cause a careful person to hesitate before acting in matters of importance to himself/herself.

Reasonable Person - A phrase used to denote a hypothetical person who exercises the qualities of attention, knowledge, intelligence, and judgment that society requires of its members for the protection of their own interest and the interests of others. This term is commonly used in torts, where the test of negligence is based on either a failure to do something that a reasonable person, guided by considerations that ordinarily regulate conduct, would do, or on the doing of something that a reasonable and prudent (wise) person would not do.

Reasonable Suspicion - Level of suspicion required to justify law enforcement investigation, but not arrest or search. A lower level of suspicion or evidence than probable cause. An officer has reasonable suspicion when the officer is aware of specific, articulable facts, together with rational inferences from those facts, which, when judged objectively, would lead a reasonable person to believe that criminal activity occurred or was occurring.

Rebut - To introduce evidence disproving other evidence previously given or reestablishing the credibility of challenged evidence.

Rebuttal - Evidence that is offered by a party after he has rested his case and after the opponent has rested in order to contradict and explain the opponent's evidence.

Rebuttal Witnesses - Witnesses introduced to explain, repel, counteract, or disprove facts given in evidence by the adverse party.

Recall Order - Court order recalling a warrant or capias (writ requiring an officer to take a named defendant into custody).

Record - All the documents and evidence plus transcripts of oral proceedings in a case.

Recusal - The voluntary action by a judge to remove himself or herself from presiding in a given case because of self-interest, bias, conflict, or prejudice. Also, the process by which a judge is disqualified from a case because a party objects.

Redirect Examination - Opportunity to present rebuttal evidence after one's evidence has been subjected to cross-examination.

Redress - To set right; to remedy; to compensate; to remove the causes of a grievance.

Referee - A person to whom the court refers a pending case to take testimony, hear the parties, and report back to the court. A referee is an officer with judicial powers who serves as an arm of the court, but whose final decision is subject to court approval. Also called "special master" "special commissioner," or "hearing officer."

Rehearing - Another hearing of a civil or criminal case or motion by the same court in which the matter was originally decided in order to bring to the court's attention an error, omission, or oversight in the first consideration.

Release - Discharge from confinement or custody.

Release On Own Recognizance - Release of a person from custody without the payment of any bail or posting of bond, upon the promise to return to court.

Remand - To send a dispute back to the court where it was originally heard. Usually it is an appellate court that remands a case for proceedings in the trial court consistent with the appellate court's ruling.

Remedy - Legal or judicial means by which a right or privilege is enforced or the violation of a right or privilege is prevented, redressed, or compensated.

Remittitur - The reduction by a judge of the damages awarded by a jury.

Removal - The transfer of a state case to federal court for trial.

Rendition - Transfer of a fugitive from the asylum state to the demanding state.

Replevin - A legal action for the recovery of a possession that has been wrongfully taken.

Reply - The response by a party to charges raised in a pleading by the other party.

Request for Production - A formal court process by which one party requests that another produce certain documents or other tangible items.

Rescission - Cancellation of a contract.

Res Judicata - A thing or matter already decided by a court. A final judgment on the merits is conclusive as to the rights of the parties and is an absolute bar to a later action involving the same claim, demand, or cause of action. Res judicata bars relitigation of the same cause of action between the same parties where there is a prior judgment. By comparison, collateral estoppel bars relitigation of a particular issue or determinative fact. Compare Collateral Estoppel.

Respondent - The person against whom an appeal is taken. See Petitioner.

Rest - A party is said to rest or rest its case when it has presented all the evidence it intends to offer.

Restitution - Either financial reimbursement to the victim or community service imposed by the court for a crime committed.

Retainer - Act of the client in employing the attorney or counsel; also denotes the fee which the client pays when he/she retains the attorney.

Return of service - A certificate of affidavit by the person who has served process upon a party to an action, reflecting the date and place of service.

Reversal - An action of a higher court in setting aside or revoking a lower court decision.

Reversible Error - An error during a trial or hearing sufficiently harmful to justify reversing the judgment of a lower court.

Revocable Trust - A trust that the grantor may change or revoke.

Revocation (of Driver's License) - Judicial termination of a driver's license and privilege to drive after conviction of DWI. The license shall not be renewed or restored for the duration of the revocation, except that an application for a new license may be presented and acted upon by the division after the expiration of at least one year after date of revocation. This kind of revocation is distinguished from an administrative revocation, in which the Motor Vehicle Division may terminate a driver's license for up to one year.

Revoke - To cancel or nullify a legal document.

Robbery - Felonious taking of another's property, from his or her person or immediate presence and against his or her will, by means of force or fear.

Rules of Evidence - Standards governing whether evidence in civil or criminal case is admissible.

S

Satisfaction of Judgment - Payment of all monies determined to be owed pursuant to a court judgment.

Seal - The Clerk of Court symbol of authenticity.

Search - Examination of a person's house or other building or premises, or of his person, or vehicle, with a view to discovery of contraband, illicit or stolen property, or some evidence of guilt to be used in the prosecution of a criminal action.

Search Warrant - A written order issued by a judge that directs a law enforcement officer to search a specific area for a specific piece of evidence.

Secured Debt - In collection or bankruptcy proceedings, a debt is secured if the debtor gave the creditor a right to repossess the property or goods used as collateral.

Self Defense - Claim that an act otherwise criminal was legally justifiable because it was necessary to protect a person or property from the threat or action of another.

Self-Incrimination (privilege against) - The constitutional right of people to refuse to give testimony against themselves that could subject them to criminal prosecution. The right is guaranteed in the Fifth Amendment to the U.S. Constitution. Asserting the right is often referred to as "Taking the Fifth."

Self-Proving Will - A will whose validity does not have to be testified to in court by the witnesses to it, since the witnesses executed an affidavit reflecting proper execution of the will prior to the maker's death.

Sentence - The punishment ordered by a court for a defendant convicted of a crime. A concurrent sentence means that two or more sentences would run at the same time. A consecutive sentence means that two or more sentences would run one after another.

Sentence Report - A document containing background material on a convicted person. It is prepared to guide the judge in the imposition of a sentence. Sometimes called a pre-sentence investigation.

Sequester - To separate. Sometimes juries are separated from outside influences during their deliberations. For example, this may occur during a highly publicized trial.

Sequestration of Witnesses - Keeping all witnesses (except plaintiff and defendant) out of the courtroom except for their time on the stand, and cautioning them not to discuss their testimony with other witnesses. Also called exclusion of witnesses. This prevents a witness from being influenced by the testimony of a prior witness.

Service - The delivery of a legal document, or of a requirement to appear in court, by an officially authorized person in accordance with the formal requirements of the applicable laws. Service is required, unless waived, for complaints, summonses, or subpoenas, to notify a person of a lawsuit or other legal action taken against him/her.

Settlement - An agreement between the parties disposing of a lawsuit.

Settlor - The person who sets up a trust. Also called the grantor or trustor.

附录二
常用法律英语词汇及术语

Severance - The separation of offenses or defendants into different trials.

Show Cause Order - Court order requiring a person to appear and show why some action should not be taken.

Sidebar - A conference between the judge and lawyers, usually in the courtroom, out of earshot of the jury and spectators.

Slander - False and defamatory spoken words tending to harm another's reputation, business or means of livelihood. Slander is spoken defamation; libel is published.

Sovereign Immunity - The doctrine that the government, state or federal, is immune to lawsuit unless it gives its consent, generally through legislation.

Special Damages - Damages that are the actual, but not necessary, consequence of a breach of contract or injury. In contract law, special damages must have been reasonably foreseeable and must flow directly and immediately from the breach, or they are not enforceable.

Specific Performance - A remedy by which a court orders a person who has breached an agreement to perform specifically what he or she has agreed to do. Specific performance is ordered when damages alone would be inadequate compensation.

Speedy Trial - A rule of law wherein the defendant must be brought to trial within 180 days.

Spendthrift Trust - A trust set up for the benefit of someone whom the grantor believes would be incapable of managing his/her own financial affairs.

Standing - The legal right to bring a lawsuit. Only a person with some legally recognized interest at stake has standing to bring a lawsuit.

Stare Decisis - The doctrine that courts will follow principles of law laid down in previous cases. Similar to precedent.

Statement - A writing made by a person and signed or otherwise adopted or approved by such person; any mechanical, electrical or other recording or a transcription thereof, which is a recital of an oral utterance; and stenographic or written statements or notes which are in substance recitals of an oral statement.

Statute - Law passed by a legislative body declaring rights and duties, or commanding or prohibiting certain conduct.

Statute of Frauds - Law which requires that certain documents be in writing, such as leases for more than one year. Under the UCC, contracts for the sale of goods for more than $500 must be in writing to be enforced.

Statute of Limitations - The time within which a plaintiff must begin a lawsuit (in civil cases) or a prosecutor must bring charges (in criminal cases). There are different statutes of limitations at both the federal and state levels for different kinds of lawsuits or crimes.

Statutory Construction - Process by which a court seeks to interpret the meaning and scope of legislation.

Statutory Law - The body of law enacted by the legislative branch of government, as distinguished from case law or common law.

Stay - A court order halting a judicial proceeding.

Stipulation - An agreement by attorneys on both sides of a civil or criminal case about some aspect of the case; e.g., to extend the time to answer, to adjourn the trial date, or to admit certain facts at the trial.

Strict Liability Statutes - Statutes criminalizing specific conduct without regard to the actor's intent. The only question for a judge or jury in a strict-liability case is whether the defendant did the prohibited act.

Strike - Highlighting evidence, in the record of case, that has been improperly offered and will not be relied upon.

Sua Sponte - A Latin phrase which means on one's own behalf, voluntary, without prompting or suggestion.

Subject Matter Jurisdiction - Power of a court to hear the type of case that is before it. Example: a municipal court has subject matter jurisdiction for cases involving violation of that municipality's ordinances, but does not have subject matter jurisdiction over felonies.

Subpoena - A process directing a witness to appear and give testimony at a certain time and in a certain place.

Subpoena Duces Tecum - A court order commanding a witness to bring certain documents or records to court.

Summary Judgment - A decision made on the basis of statements and evidence presented for the record without a trial. It is used when there is no dispute as to the material facts of the case, and one party is entitled to judgment as a matter of law.

Summons - A document signed by a deputy clerk ordering a person to appear before the court to respond to a complaint.

Support Trust - A trust that instructs the trustee to spend only as much income and principal (the assets held in the trust) as needed for the beneficiary's support.

Suppress - To forbid the use of evidence at a trial because it is improper or was improperly obtained. See also exclusionary rule.

Supra - Latin for above.

Surety - One who signs a bond and guarantees to pay money if the defendant fails to appear in court as ordered.

Surety Bond - A bond purchased at the expense of the estate to insure the executor's proper performance.

Survivorship - Another name for joint tenancy, in which one owner becomes entitled to property because he or she has survived all other owners.

Suspended Sentence - Postponed execution of sentence; sentence is imposed, and execution of sentence is suspended, postponed, or stayed for a period and on conditions set by the judge.

Suspension (of driver's license) - The driver's license and privilege to drive are temporarily withdrawn, but only during the period of such suspension. No reapplication is necessary to obtain license.

Sustain - A court ruling upholding an objection or a motion.

Sworn Complaint Affidavit - A sworn, witnessed complaint filed with the Clerk of the Court.

T

Temporary Relief - Any form of action by a court granting one of the parties an order designed to protect its interest pending further action by the court.

Temporary Restraining Order - A judge's order forbidding certain actions until a full hearing can be held. Usually of short duration. Often referred to as a TRO.

Testamentary Capacity - The legal ability to make a will.

Testamentary Trust - A trust set up by a will. This trust becomes effective only upon the death of the testator.

Testator - Person who makes a will (female: testatrix).

Testimony - The evidence given by a witness under oath. It does not include evidence from documents and other physical evidence.

Third Party - A person, business, organization or government agency not actively involved in a legal proceeding, agreement, or transaction, but affected by it.

Third-Party Claim - An action by the defendant that brings a third party into a lawsuit.

Time served - Actual number of days already served in jail on a charge or offense before conviction.

Title - Legal ownership of property, usually real property or automobiles.

Tort - An injury or wrong committed on the person or property of another. A tort is an infringement on the rights of an individual, but not founded in a contract. The most common tort action is a suit for personal and/or property damages sustained in an automobile accident.

Transcript - A written, word-for-word record of what was said, either in a proceeding such as a trial or during some other conversation, as in a transcript of a hearing or oral deposition.

Transfer cases - Cases going from one court or one jurisdiction to another.

Trial - Examination of any issue of fact or law before a competent court to determine the rights of the parties.

Trial by Jury - Trial by a body of persons selected from the citizens of a particular district and brought before the court where they are sworn to try one or more questions of fact and determine them by their verdict.

Trial de Novo - A retrial in district court that is conducted as if no trial had occurred in the lower court.

True Bill - A finding by a grand jury that there is sufficient evidence to warrant a criminal charge; allows trial to proceed. An indictment.

True Copy - An exact copy of a written instrument.

Trust - A legal device used to manage real or personal property, established by one person (the grantor or settlor) for the benefit of another (the beneficiary). A third person (the trustee) or the grantor manages the trust.

Trust Agreement or Declaration - The legal document that sets up a living trust. Testamentary trusts are set up in a will.

Trustee - The person or institution that manages the property put in trust.

Trustor - Grantor, settlor; one who establishes a trust.

U

UCC - Uniform Commercial Code. The UCC applies to the sale of movable goods to or by a merchant. New Mexico's UCC statutes are encoded at NMSA 1978, §§ 55-1-101 to -12-109.

Unenforceable Contract - A valid contract is unenforceable when some defense exists that is extraneous to the formation of the contract, such as when the contract violates the Statute of Frauds or the Statute of Limitations has passed.

Unjust Enrichment - Occurs when a person has unfairly gained at the expense of another (such as by mistake), and principles of justice and equity require the person to return or pay for the property or benefits received.

Unlawful Detainer - An unjustifiable retention of real estate without the consent of the owner or other person entitled to its possession; may occur when a tenant refuses to leave premises after the right of occupancy has ended.

Unlawful Search - Examination or inspection of premises or persons without authority of the law and in violation of the immunity from unreasonable search and seizure under the Fourth Amendment to the U.S. Constitution and Article II, Section 10 of the New Mexico Constitution.

Unsecured - In collection or bankruptcy proceedings, a debt or a claim is unsecured if there is no collateral, or to the extent the value of collateral is less than the amount of the debt.

Usury - Charging a higher interest rate or higher fees than the law allows.

V

Vacate - To set aside, as a judgment.

Venire - A writ summoning persons to court to act as jurors, also refers to the people summoned for jury duty, as in the "jury venire" or "jury panel."

Venue - The place in which prosecution is brought; venue may be in the county of the defendant's residence or in the county in which the offense is alleged to have been committed.

Vested - Fixed; accrued; settled; absolute.

Verdict - The findings of a judge or jury at the end of the trial.

Void Contract - A contract that does not have any legal effect and cannot be enforced under any circumstances. For example, a contract to commit an illegal act is void.

Voidable Contract - A valid contract that a party may cancel upon request. For example, a contract made by a minor is voidable by the minor or his or her legal guardian.

Voir Dire - A form of questioning designed to establish the qualifications of prospective jurors to serve in a case.

W

Waive - To give up a known right voluntarily. Example: To give up the right to an attorney.

Waiver - In extradition proceedings, a form signed before a judge whereby a defendant voluntarily submits to pick-up by a foreign jurisdiction, waiving his/her rights as guaranteed under the Constitution.

Waiver of Immunity - A means authorized by statute by which a witness, before testifying or producing evidence, may relinquish the right to refuse to testify against himself or herself, thereby making it possible for his or her testimony to be used against him or her in future proceedings.

Warrant - Most commonly, a court order authorizing law enforcement officers to make an arrest or conduct a search. An affidavit seeking a warrant must establish probable cause by detailing the facts upon which the request is based.

Warrantless Search - Examination of a person or premises without first obtaining a warrant, which may be lawful under such limited circumstances as a domestic violence situation, emergency, hot pursuit, consent, or threat of immediate removal of contraband.

Warranty - A legal promise that certain facts are true.

Will - A legal declaration that disposes of a person's property when that person dies.

Without Prejudice - A claim or cause dismissed without prejudice may be the subject of a new lawsuit.

With Prejudice - Applied to orders of judgment dismissing a case, meaning that the plaintiff is forever barred from bringing a lawsuit on the same claim or cause.

Witness - A person who testifies to what he/she has seen, heard, or otherwise experienced. Also, a person who observes the signing of a will and is competent to testify that it is the will-maker's intended last will and testament.

Writ - A judicial order directing a person to do something.

Writ of Attachment - A writ of the court ordering the sheriff to seize or hold a debtor's property and bring the property before the court.

Writ of Certiorari - An order by the appellate court used when the court has the discretion on whether or not to hear an appeal.

Writ of Mandamus - A writ to compel performance of one's responsibilities as set forth by law.

Writ of Prohibition - A writ used by a superior court to prevent an inferior court from exceeding its jurisdiction.

Writ of Superintending Control - A writ issued to prevent a gross miscarriage of justice by correcting the erroneous ruling of a lower court that is acting within its jurisdiction but is making mistakes of law or is acting in willful disregard of the law. The writ is issued when there is no appeal or when an appeal cannot provide adequate relief.

X

Xml - Acronym for Extensible Markup Language. XML is an information format that can be understood by virtually all computer users, regardless of their particular platforms. XML is used to share information in a consistent manner.

Xss - Cross-Site Scripting (XXS) refers to a kind of computer security vulnerability, most often found in web applications, whereby malicious web programmers are able to inject code into websites viewed by external users. Programmers exploiting these type of vulnerabilities can gain access to sensitive information on the external user's computer, and even take control of the computer's functions.

Xw abbr - Ex-warrants.

Y

Youthful offender - A young person (as one within a statutorily specified age range) who commits a crime but is granted special status entitling him or her to a more lenient punishment (as one involving probation or confinement in a special youth correctional facility) than would otherwise be available compare juvenile delinquent, status offender NOTE: Young individuals who are no longer juveniles may be categorized as youthful offenders. Youthful offender treatment is generally designed to free a young person from the negative consequences of being convicted and punished as an adult, in the hope that he or she will be rehabilitated. Factors in the determination of youthful offender status include the crime and the criminal history of the individual.

Year-and-a-day rule - A common-law rule that relieves a defendant of responsibility for homicide if the victim lives for more than one year and one day after being injured *NOTE: The year-and-a-day rule, which dates from at least 1278, is frequently criticized as anachronistic since modern medicine makes pinpointing cause of death easier than it was formerly. However, the rule still exists or is reflected in the law of some jurisdictions.*

Z

Zone of danger - The area within which one is in actual physical peril from the negligent conduct of another person *NOTE: Some jurisdictions require that a bystander who witnesses a direct injury to another can only recover for negligent infliction of emotional distress if he or she was also in the zone of danger—that is, in actual danger of physical injury.*

Zone of privacy - An area or aspect of life that is held to be protected from intrusion by a specific constitutional guarantee (as of the right to be secure in one's person, house, papers, or effects against unreasonable searches or seizures) or is the object of an expectation of privacy

Zoning - The division of certain areas in a community into various categories for permission to build, or not to build, certain types of structures. For example, a certain area may be zoned for residential structures only, while another area permits business structures only.